# 60
# REMARKABLE
# BUILDINGS

### of the National Trust

# 60 REMARKABLE BUILDINGS

## of the National Trust

DR ELIZABETH GREEN
INTRODUCTION BY GEORGE CLARKE

*With entries by Frances Bailey, Rupert Goulding, James Grasby,*
*Sally-Anne Huxtable, Mark Newman, Stephen Ponder, Lucy Porten,*
*George Roberts, Simon Robertshaw and Emma Slocombe*

# Contents

# Introduction by George Clarke

One of my earliest memories is of looking out of my bedroom window and seeing a strange architectural structure, high up on a hill, far away in the distance. I must have been around four years of age – so very young indeed. I couldn't work out what it was. It had such a mystery to it. I could have asked my parents what it was, but for reasons I've never worked out, I never did.

From the angle I was looking at it, it had the profile and silhouette of two giant, American-style trashcans (like the ones I'd seen on the American cartoon *Top Cat*), with vertical flutes and triangular tops. I genuinely thought this might be the place where they took all the rubbish from the town to get rid of it.

What I was actually looking at was Penshaw Monument. This is no ordinary building. Its design is based on the Temple of Hephaestus in Athens – a tetrastyle temple of the Doric order. Why on earth was a Greek-style temple built on a hill in the post-industrial city of Sunderland?

Penshaw Monument is actually a Grade I listed Victorian monument, built in 1844–5 to commemorate John Lambton, 1st Earl of Durham, and it has been owned and maintained by the National Trust since 1939. What is so powerful about it is that everyone in the city absolutely loves 'Pensha'. And when I say 'love', I really mean it. It's a member of our extended northern family. It appears on the crest of our beloved football club, people propose in front of it, ashes are scattered beside it and mythical stories are told about it.

In many ways it symbolises and reflects so much about this particular part of the North East and the character of the people who live here. It is a tough, gritty and resilient structure, but it also has a sublime beauty to it. It is a building that had a profound effect on my life and it was certainly one of the first pieces of architecture that inspired me to become an architect. It makes me laugh now that as a four-year-old I mistook the two triangular, classical pediments (which sat perfectly side by side from my viewpoint) for trashcan lids, and the gaps between the Doric columns for the flutes on the face of two giant trashcan drums! Fortunately, my observational skills got better with age.

*Opposite* · George Clarke visiting the Rock Houses at Kinver Edge, Staffordshire, while filming *George Clarke's National Trust Unlocked* in 2020.
*Frontispiece* · Fountains Abbey, North Yorkshire (pages 26–9)
*Pages 4–5* · Ickworth, Suffolk (pages 116–17)

Many years later, in 2020, during the first Covid lockdown, Channel 4 asked me whether I could make a television series that would somehow comply with all the tough government restrictions then in place. That very same day, I'd seen in the news that the National Trust had been forced to close its houses to the public. Every year, 27 million visits are made to the Trust's buildings and gardens, but all the visits to its historic properties would come to a dramatic halt with Covid-19. Out of this heart-breaking situation, however, came the most serendipitous opportunity: would the National Trust be willing to unlock its closed doors to allow me to explore some of its wonderful places, so everyone in Britain could experience them through the magic of television while they were being told to stay at home? Thankfully, the Trust said yes.

Over the next few months I lived in a bubble with a very small filming team, travelling around Britain to shoot six of the most beautiful but surreal episodes of television I've ever made – *George Clarke's National Trust Unlocked*. There were no people around, no cars, no aeroplanes overhead to upset the soundman, and we had access to areas of these remarkable buildings that the public had never seen before.

Each episode featured an unusual building (like the Kinver Edge Rock Houses in Staffordshire, which were the last troglodyte dwellings in England), a National Trust garden (like the beautifully architectural and formal 17th-century water gardens at Westbury Court in Gloucestershire), a National Trust walk (like the geologically stunning Studland Bay and Old Harry Rocks in Dorset) and finally a National Trust grand house (including my favourite National Trust building of all time, Cragside in Northumberland). I also have to mention that we filmed at Washington Old Hall, Tyne and Wear, the ancestral home of

George Washington, the first president of the United States, which I visited regularly while training as an architectural apprentice from the age of 16. The earliest parts of this historic house date back to the mid-13th century. By the standards of the National Trust (and I think they would agree), Washington Old Hall is a relatively modest, fairly unassuming building, and we could never quite understand, as young kids, why American tourists would arrive by the coach-load each summer to see it. Today, of course, we can grasp its powerful historical significance.

To this day, all of the people who worked on the *National Trust Unlocked* series feel privileged to have been a part of it. It is no exaggeration for me to say that it was one of the most memorable and magical experiences of my life, and I'll always be thankful to the National Trust for allowing me to make it. The entire series ended with me proudly doing a piece to camera while walking along the top of the entablature of our northern family member, Penshaw Monument.

The National Trust cares for over 10,000 buildings in the UK. It is also the nation's largest farm-owner, with nearly 250,000 hectares of land and more than 1,300 tenant farmers. How on earth Dr Elizabeth Green and her fellow writers have had the discipline to select just 60 remarkable buildings from such an enormous

portfolio to write this beautiful book is beyond me – but what a selection they have made! Whether large or small, urban or rural, ancient or modern, the stories that these buildings tell us are absolutely fascinating.

Some of the buildings that jump out of these pages for me include The Crown Liquor

*Below* • Washington Old Hall, Tyne and Wear

Saloon in Belfast, which was championed by one of my all-time building-saving heroes, Sir John Betjeman, and purchased by the National Trust in 1978. There is 251 Menlove Avenue, an unassuming semi-detached house in the suburbs of Liverpool, where a young lad lived with his aunt and uncle between the ages of six and 23. That boy's name was John Lennon.

Being a fan of amazing and unusual small spaces, I have to mention the humble Shack at Mottistone Manor on the Isle of Wight, designed by architects John Seely and Paul Paget in the mid-1930s to provide an escape from the stresses of city life. Then there is the brilliantly bonkers Obelisk Lodge at Nostell in West Yorkshire, designed by the Neo-classical architect Robert Adam in 1776-7. For me, Adam was an architectural rock star, something that is clearly reflected in this small pavilion building that is part Tuscan temple, part Egyptian pyramid.

I absolutely love the National Trust and that love grew to another level when I decided at the age of 12 to become an architect. So this introduction is the perfect opportunity for me to personally thank the National Trust for bringing so much joy to my life. It is a fantastic organisation that educates, inspires and allows us to enjoy so much of the great outdoors. Without the Trust we would have lost so much of our architectural heritage and picturesque landscape, so it is vital we do everything we can to support it.

I just hope that I live long enough to make the most of my lifetime membership and see many, many more beautiful buildings, gardens, walks, structures and monuments, including the 60 remarkable buildings in this book, many of which I've not seen – yet.

Enjoy!

George Clarke

# An exceptional collection

The National Trust cares for over 10,000 historic buildings, more than 300 of which are open to the public. They represent 900 years of architectural design, from Horton Court in Gloucestershire, built c.1185, to the Giant's Causeway Visitor Centre in County Antrim, completed as recently as 2012. This astonishing collection includes urban and rural, industrial and domestic buildings, places of spirituality and faith, life and death. They are vast and intimate, and they speak of wealth, poverty and human endeavour. They showcase the richly varied regional building styles, materials and techniques found across England, Wales and Northern Ireland, and embody skills, traditions and knowledge passed down over many generations.

Vast uplands fringed with scattered farmsteads; ancient field patterns and vibrant village communities connected by routes trodden over thousands of years; great buildings that echo and breathe the voices of past lives – they are all tangible reminders of our intangible heritage.

*Opposite* · Purchased in 1896 for £10, Alfriston Clergy House in East Sussex was the first building saved for the nation by the National Trust.

The names of many of our greatest architects are associated with National Trust buildings – Robert Smythson, William Talman, Sir John Vanbrugh, Robert Adam, James Paine, John Nash, Thomas Telford, Thomas Hopper, William Burges, George Frederick Bodley, Sir Edwin Lutyens and Ernö Goldfinger. Together, the buildings of the Trust comprise an exceptional collection.

It is only from the Middle Ages that domestic buildings survive in substantial numbers. The bloody revolt of Owain Glyndŵr in 1400–9 witnessed a scorched-earth policy across Wales and the border counties. To date, no Welsh house, other than castles and ecclesiastical houses, has been dated to pre-1400. Aberconwy House in Conwy (1419) is part of the phase of major post-Glyndŵr rebuilding.

England's medieval architecture survives in greater quantities: the villages of Lacock in Wiltshire and Lavenham in Suffolk; manorial dwellings such as Lower Brockhampton in Herefordshire (early 15th century) and Ightham Mote in Kent (14th century); and castles such as Sizergh (15th century) in Cumbria and Dunster (13th century) in Somerset. Northern Ireland, like Northumberland and Scotland, tended towards compact, defensive towers, like Carra Castle in County Antrim (14th century).

*Above* · The south-west corner of Ightham Mote, an outstanding 14th-century moated manor house in Kent. *Opposite* · The grand Palladian chapel at Gibside, Tyne and Wear, designed by James Paine in 1760.

At this time, the designers of buildings were not known as architects but as master masons, and their names are generally not recorded. The Welsh term for architect is still *pensaer*, literally translating as 'head mason'. Master James of St George, master mason for the North Wales castles of Edward I, is thought to have designed Chirk Castle, Wrexham, built for Roger Mortimer between 1295 and 1310.

Sometimes, the ancient origins of buildings become disguised over time, hidden beneath later layers. But tell-tale hints survive, such as the riot of medieval cusped bracing at Lytes Cary Manor in Somerset, or the magnificent smoke-blackened oak timbers at Welsh hall house Egryn, Gwynedd (*c*.1510).

sophistication and finesse – not to mention sheer acreage of glass.

French and Dutch fashions, introduced by returning diplomats and merchants, heralded much ornamentation, the use of contrasting building materials – as seen at Ham House in Richmond (c.1610) and Blickling Hall in Norfolk (c.1619–27) – and patterns echoed both internally and in formal gardens such as Erddig, Wrexham (early 18th century) and Hanbury Hall, Worcestershire (c.1701).

Kingston Lacy in Dorset (1663–5) and its lost sister house at Coleshill in Oxfordshire (also by Sir Roger Pratt, c.1650), Tredegar House in Newport (c.1670) and Belton House, Lincolnshire (mason William Stanton, 1685–8) all display the characteristic hipped roofs, deep swept eaves, tall chimney stacks and pleasingly symmetrical winged floor plans that typify the later 17th-century 'Restoration' house.

The 18th century brought a new flourish to architectural design. The principal influence was 16th-century Italian architect Andrea Palladio. Palladio's Venetian bridge design (c.1556 but never executed) was recreated at Stowe in Buckinghamshire (1738) and Prior Park in Somerset (1750s). James Paine's delectable chapel-mortuary at Gibside, Tyne and Wear (1760) hinted at Palladio's Villa Rotonda (c.1567), and Paine and Adam came together at Kedleston Hall in Derbyshire (1759–65) to create one of the

The cataclysmic shifts in power that accompanied the reigns of Henry VIII and Elizabeth I were mirrored in stylistic developments in architecture from the 1530s through to c.1610. Undoubtedly the superstar of the time was Bess of Hardwick's architect Robert Smythson, whose name has also been associated with both Gawthorpe Hall in Lancashire (1600–5) and Chastleton House in Oxfordshire (1603–18), although both fall short of Hardwick, Derbyshire (1590–7) in

great houses of the period, building on Matthew Brettingham's designs, which were inspired by Palladio's Villa Mocenigo (c.1554).

Influenced by the grand tour, landscapes at Stourhead in Wiltshire (c.1725) and Shugborough in Staffordshire (mid-18th century) were filled with miniature temples, reflecting the Arcadian vision captured in the paintings of Claude Lorrain and Nicolas Poussin, and the architecture of Italy and Greece. The style was embraced by gentry and aristocracy, who rushed to create their country houses in the likeness of the Parthenon in Athens. However, the passion for porticos had quietly begun a whole century earlier when England's first was created from painted timber and stuccoed brick c.1654 at The Vyne in Hampshire, a previously handsome Tudor palace. Many of these great houses, including Vanbrugh's Seaton Delaval Hall in Northumberland (c.1718–28) are illustrated in Colen Campbell's *Vitruvius Britannicus* (1715–25).

The Industrial Revolution, from the late 18th century, was harnessed by the textile industry with the construction of mills such as Quarry Bank in Cheshire, along with grand homes for their owners, and over the following decades railways, canals and roads transformed the movement of goods and people. Housing was built in huge quantities for workers flocking to cities such as Manchester, Cardiff, Belfast and Birmingham.

Landscapes were transformed and society shifted from an agricultural subsistence and artisan economy to one of mechanised mass-production. The model farm at Shugborough (1806) had water-driven threshing machines, while that at Coleshill, built in the 1850s, used a system of rails to move produce around the site. Many farming communities changed the ways in which they worked. For example, Ysbyty Ifan community mill and drying kiln in Conwy (c.1870) was located in the heart of the village to enable cooperation in the processing of corn.

The upland pastoral farms that make up a large proportion of the Trust's rural architecture are principally vernacular buildings, for example the Lake District farmsteads so beloved of Beatrix Potter. However, estate designers such as James Wyatt at Llandygai for the Penrhyn Estate introduced consistency of design and a picturesque air to villages such as Cambo on the Wallington estate in Northumberland, complete with school, church and dolphin water-spout.

Rural buildings, represented in this book by the Townend bank barn of 1666 in Cumbria and the early 18th-century Treleddyd Fawr in Pembrokeshire, reflect the landscapes in which they lie – their materials, form and function responding directly to local conditions. The

*Right* · Levant Mine and its steam-driven beam engine, built in 1840, sit on the cliffs of Cornwall's 'Tin Coast'.

*Above* · Built at the height of the Cold War in the 1950s and 1960s, the modernist structures of the atomic research facility at Orford Ness, Suffolk, are gradually being reclaimed by nature (pages 192–5).

their own way and uniquely describe the history of their own locality.

### Selecting 60 buildings

The National Trust is in the business of caring for remarkable places, so narrowing a selection down to 60 has been a challenge, albeit a delightful one. It was important to showcase not just the glittering megastars of the architectural firmament, such as Kedleston Hall in Derbyshire and Knole in Kent, but some of the less well-known

selection could have included the 17th-century timber-framed donkey wheel at Saddlescombe Farm in West Sussex, the stone kelp houses of Strangford Lough, County Down, or the Levant tin-mine structures on the wild north Cornish coast. These structures are all remarkable in

buildings whose contribution to our understanding of social and political history is nevertheless incredibly important, such as Springhill in County Londonderry, Branscombe Forge in Devon and The Needles batteries on the Isle of Wight.

Thus, Hardwick and Seaton Delaval become happy bedfellows with the Isle of Wight's Mottistone Shack. The selection is not proportionally representative of the Trust's collection of buildings. If it were, this would be a book of cottages and cow-houses.

## Caring for amazing architecture

When it was created in 1895, the Trust's principal purpose was to protect outdoor spaces at a time when city air was thick with pollution and access to green space was limited. The first building to be saved was Alfriston Clergy House (*c.*1405), a 'Wealden' house in East Sussex rescued in 1896 and bought for £10. In the ensuing decades, a torrent of endangered buildings would come into the care of this remarkable organisation.

Anyone who has dipped into the diaries of James Lees-Milne, secretary of the Country Houses Committee of the National Trust during the 1930s and 1940s, will understand the gravity of the situation facing the owners of many ancient houses and estates in the aftermath of war and economic decline. Soaring death duties and huge loss of workforce saw large numbers of our greatest country houses falling into disrepair and historic families forced to sell their art, heirlooms and land. The National Trust Acts of 1937 and 1939 enabled the Trust to take on estates and open them to the public, thereby returning the benefit to the nation and bringing a halt to the disintegration of this important part of our heritage.

Buildings are a precious record of changing ways of life, social division, political and religious struggle. Estate farms and cottages provide homes and livelihoods for future generations, and the Trust works closely with tenants and local communities to ensure that they are sustainable, vibrant and environmentally responsible. Today, although it does occasionally take on major houses (such as Seaton Delaval in 2009 and Stoneywell, Leicestershire in 2012), the Trust's focus is on addressing the challenges presented to our buildings, landscapes and habitats by climate change, and on ensuring that our places are cared for and contribute to the wellbeing of all.

We hope you enjoy this book and that it inspires you to visit one or two remarkable buildings of the National Trust.

Dr Elizabeth Green
*Senior National Curator for Architectural History and for Wales, National Trust*

*Overleaf* · The balcony overlooking the garden at The Homewood, Esher, Surrey (pages 188–91).

# 60 REMARKABLE BUILDINGS

# A rare Norman gem

Historic buildings often present us with the delightful challenge of unpicking their multi-layered histories and revealing the stories behind their architecture. In the case of Horton Court this is a remarkably long timeline. At its heart is a hall dating from *c.*1185, only a few generations after the Norman conquest, making it one of England's earliest houses and the National Trust's oldest inhabited building.

One of only a handful of houses surviving from the Norman period, this little hall is a real gem. Like most ancient buildings, it has been adapted by generations of occupants to suit their needs, but it still bears the hallmarks of Norman architecture: small, round-headed doors and windows, embellished with chunky chevron decoration and round shafts with scalloped trumpet capitals.

The two doors stand opposite each other and would have marked the screens, or cross-passage, separating the 'high' end of the hall from the lower. The high end would have been the focal point, perhaps with a raised platform or dais. The walls would have been painted or possibly hung with cloth, and the floor covered with a mixture of dried grasses and fragrant strewing herbs such as sweet woodruff or rosemary. Horton was built for the priest

of the parish, Robert de Bellafago (d.1219), who is first noted as prebendary of Horton in 1142.

However, the bulk of the house was added c.1521 for William Knight (c.1475–1547). He was ambassador to kings Henry VII and VIII, attended the Field of the Cloth of Gold, and negotiated with the Pope to secure the divorce between Henry VIII and Catherine of Aragon. He travelled widely in Italy, from Ferrara, where he studied at the university, to Rome, and it was surely this that inspired his taste in architecture.

Horton's importance is reflected in the succession of priests who held it: three became cardinals, two became archbishops and eleven became bishops, and many of their arms still decorate the building. In particular, though, it is the Italian-inspired Renaissance designs of William Knight's 1521 house, exceptionally early and comparable with detailing at Hampton Court Palace, that crown Horton as a truly remarkable building. EG

**Horton Court, Gloucestershire** · Norman and Renaissance hall · *c.1185, c.1521, restored 1884* · *Cotswold stone, stone-tile roof* · *Bequest, 1946*

# From humble beginnings

Living in poverty and obedience, Fountains Abbey's monks expressed their appreciation of God's glory and their dedication to his worship through their magnificent buildings. Twelve dissident monks and their prior, looking for a more austere and worshipful life, left York's St Mary's Abbey to found Fountains Abbey on St Stephen's Day (26 December) 1132. They sheltered under an elm tree as they first built a small timber church.

Set around that little kernel, they raised successively larger stone churches as the monastic community grew. The nave reached its present size by around 1160, the choir by 1200 and the broad nine-altared chancel by 1240. Appended to the church were three ranges of domestic buildings around a central cloister, the hub around which the monastic day revolved. Most of the buildings we see today, except for the distinctive bell tower, were complete by 1250, accommodating perhaps up to 400 lay brothers and 160 choir monks. Necessary repairs completed in the 1480s were ornamented with portraits, rebuses (visual puns), angels and even a Green Man – in origin, a pagan woodland god.

Fountains adopted industrial-scale planning from a remarkably early date, in the 1140s, consolidating its status as the wealthiest and largest of England's Cistercian houses. One reflection of this is the suite of huge production buildings set out across the rest of the 12-acre precinct. These include Fountains Mill – the oldest in-use building owned by the National Trust – and archaeological remains, such as the recently rediscovered tannery building.

Fountains was among the last monasteries to be dissolved by King Henry VIII (1491–1547), in November 1539. Only the core of the monastery survives today, first preserved as a place of antiquarian interest and latterly as a feature of the Aislabie family's Studley Royal designed landscape – now a World Heritage Site. MN

**Fountains Abbey, North Yorkshire** · Cistercian abbey · *12th–16th centuries* · *Local sandstone, with Nidderdale marble and limestone detailing* · *Purchased, 1983*

# Witness to history

This cathedral-like space was built when Edward I (1239–1307) was building castles long since fallen into ruin. It has seen war, plague, the dissolution of monasteries and the rise and fall of royal dynasties.

With its cruciform plan and aisled interior, it closely resembles a church. It is likely to have been built by carpenters and stonemasons who were accustomed to building churches, as Great Coxwell was owned by Beaulieu Abbey and was designed to protect grain, a valuable commodity for the abbey.

Barns are easy to spot among other agricultural buildings, as they have distinctive, functional features. Ventilation slits pierce the walls, to air the grain without allowing rain to spoil it. Two large openings, roughly halfway along the building, bring cross-wind to the threshing bay, where the wheat is separated from the chaff. The ears of wheat are tossed into the air and the unwanted material is allowed to blow away, leaving the heavier grain to fall to the floor.

The rows of small, square holes running along the walls are 'putlog', or scaffolding holes. EG

**Great Coxwell, Oxfordshire** · Medieval tithe barn ·
*1292 · Rubble and dressed Cotswold stone, stone-tile roof ·*
*Mr E.E. Cook bequest, 1956*

# Defence in depth

Bodiam Castle's soaring walls rise straight out of the glassy water of its moat. It was built by Sir Edward Dalyngrigge (1346–93), knight, mercenary and member of parliament. Dalyngrigge fought in France in the Hundred Years War, amassing considerable fortunes through pillage and plunder. By 1385 the French threat saw England's efforts to defend its south coast escalate and Dalyngrigge was granted a licence to crenelate (royal permission to fortify the building).

Bodiam is a courtyard castle, with huge defensive towers at each corner. The high-status rooms, as well as kitchens and accommodation for the garrison, are protected within the curtain wall. Arrow loops surveyed the surrounding landscape, murder holes and portcullis guarded the gatehouse, and the 28 garderobes discharged into the moat.

At the end of the English Civil War, the practice of dismantling castles began. Bodiam became a romantic ruin. Having passed through the hands of several owners and seen various campaigns of work, in 1916 Bodiam was bought by Lord Curzon (1859–1925), who conducted more extensive repairs. EG

**Bodiam Castle, East Sussex** · Medieval castle · *c.1385* · *Wadhurst sandstone ashlar* · *Curzon bequest, 1925*

# Calm cloister

The soft shuffle of feet, muffled conversation and distant plainsong are easily summoned to mind beneath the golden archways of Lacock Abbey's cloister (opposite and overleaf). The cloister was a covered corridor giving sheltered access from the abbey church to domestic or administrative spaces. Surrounding a courtyard or garden, it was an intimate space for walking and talking, if allowed, or quiet contemplation. In some cases, a long handwashing basin ran along one wall, for monks or nuns to wash the dirt of outdoor tasks from their hands before heading into the abbey for prayer.

Lacock's cloister is one of the finest examples of Perpendicular architecture, where window tracery is based on parallel vertical lines and vaults are woven from intricate webs of finely moulded ribs. Where the ribs meet, we find bosses carved with flowers, foliage and faces. Of course, as with much architectural decoration in churches, it is purposefully focused on the upper reaches of the building, drawing the eye – and the mind – heavenwards.

The Abbey, an Augustinian nunnery, was founded in 1229 by Ela, Countess of Salisbury (1187–1261) and the building complex evolved over the following two centuries. The cloister dates mostly from the 15th century, towards the end of the Abbey's life. Following the Dissolution of the Monasteries in the late 1530s, Henry VIII sold the Abbey to William Sharington (c.1495–1553), who demolished the church but kept and converted a great deal otherwise: the cloister, chapter house, sacristy, warming room, dormitory, refectory, parlour, chaplain's room, kitchen, undercrofts and gateway. The medieval dormitory and refectory roofs are still in situ. All of this makes Lacock one of the most complete surviving examples of a medieval nunnery.

This beautiful space found recent fame in the Harry Potter film series. EG

**Lacock Abbey, Wiltshire** · Cloister · *14th and 15th centuries with alterations in the mid-16th century · Cotswold rubble and dressed limestone, stone-tile roof · Gift, 1944*

# Statement of status

Oxburgh, in the Norfolk Breckland, was inherited by Sir Edmund Bedingfield (1443–96) in 1476 and granted licence to crenelate by Edward IV (1442–83) in 1482. Building began soon afterwards on a handsome, brick-built house, which, while employing defensive features such as a moat and gatehouse, was designed principally as a symbol of status and would not, in reality, have repelled serious hostile activity. The house would, however, become a place of sanctuary from the late 16th century with the creation of a priest hole. The Bedingfield family held a devout Catholic faith and, at this time of religious persecution for Catholics, the harbouring of a priest was a serious offence.

Typical of high-status houses of the Tudor period, Oxburgh has a spectacular gatehouse (right), with a dramatic pair of three-storey towers framing the entrance. The gatehouse is often the main surviving element of houses of the Tudor period – tall, turreted and lavishly designed as a statement of power and demonstration of architectural taste.

The choice of brick as a building material was popular in the east of England, initially due to bricks arriving from the Netherlands as ballast in ships. By the later 15th century

it was no longer a novelty, although it was rarely used on this scale, more often reserved for ornate details such as chimneys. The bold choice of brick as the principal material at Oxburgh is a grand architectural statement, demonstrating status and self-confidence on the part of the Bedingfield family.

The house is roughly square in plan. The great gatehouse is to the north and, opposite it, across the courtyard, was the Great Hall. Once the focal point of activities at Oxburgh, it was demolished in 1775, apparently due to the cost of the repairs needed, and never replaced. The low buildings that fill the gap today are by the Gothic Revival architect J.C. Buckler (1793–1894), who carried out alterations in the 1830s, embellishing and emphasising the Gothic style of Oxburgh. A.C. Pugin illustrates Oxburgh in his *Examples of Gothic Architecture* (1831–8) but there is no evidence for him, or his more famous son A.W.N. Pugin, having made alterations to the house. A.W.N. Pugin's style and that of Buckler have strong similarities, possibly leading to this presumption. EG

**Oxburgh Hall, Norfolk** · Tudor house · *Medieval to 1870s* · *Red brick, clay-pantile roof · Gift, 1952*

# The ring of truth

Dendrochronology – tree-ring dating – has transformed the work of building detectives, allowing them to unpick the layers of timber-framed buildings and identify when each part was built. Oak was used 'green', or unseasoned, so knowing the season when a tree was felled indicates the date it was used.

The timbers in Lower Brockhampton's hall were felled between 1413 and 1441, and those of the cross wing between 1398 and 1434. It is likely that the hall, the heart of the house, was built first, followed by the chambers and withdrawing rooms, suggesting that both ranges were built early in the 15th century. Records tell us that the manor of Brockhampton was owned by Philip Domulton at this time, making him the likely creator of the house.

A buttery, pantry and kitchen were added in 1520–8 by Richard Habington and the gatehouse across the moat was built in 1545–50. A retreat from medieval communal living saw John Barneby introduce ceilings over the Great Chamber and the Great Hall in 1661–8. EG

**Lower Brockhampton, Herefordshire** · Moated medieval manor house · *1413 onwards* · *Timber-framed with wattle and daub infill and brick chimneys, clay-tile roof* · *Bequest, 1946*

# Surmounted by leopards

Knole is one of the great country houses of England. Located in a medieval deer park just off the busy high street of Sevenoaks, the approach to the house up a tree-lined winding drive can feel like stepping back in time. Often likened in size to a town rather than a house, the roofs alone cover 6.7 acres. Flanked on four sides by towering walls of Kentish ragstone, its entrance front is surmounted by curved gables topped with heraldic Sackville leopards standing either side of an imposing gatehouse. A climb up the gatehouse spiral staircase is rewarded by the sight of a vast roofscape of gabled ranges and chimneys arranged around a series of courtyards that reveal the structure of the medieval palace at its heart.

The early manor house at Knole was purchased by Thomas Bourchier (c.1411–86), Archbishop of Canterbury, in 1456 and transformed into his palace. It was extended under successive archbishops and by Henry VIII, before being purchased in 1603 by Thomas Sackville, 1st Earl of Dorset (c.1536–1608), cousin and Lord High Treasurer to Elizabeth I (1533–1603). Sackville employed master craftsmen from the King's Works to remodel his house. Using the footprint of the medieval building and incorporating the old Great Hall,

chapel and tithe barn, in under a decade Knole was transformed into a Renaissance palace. Its formal interiors were lavishly decorated with ornate plasterwork, carving and painted schemes, supported behind the scenes by an extensive network of kitchens, a dairy and brewery, stables, workshops and wood yard.

Later generations gently modified and repaired the building, but Thomas Sackville's Jacobean masterpiece survives, largely as he intended, 400 years later. Today, the house embodies an atmospheric faded grandeur, its long galleries, winding staircases, staterooms and attics encrusted with heraldic beasts and mythological figures and surfaces that carry the patina of centuries. ES

**Knole, Kent** · Renaissance palace · *1456 onwards · Kentish ragstone with brick chimneys, clay-tile roof · Gift, 1947*

# Transcending symmetry

Little Moreton is one of the most spectacular timber-framed buildings in England. The building phases were carried out by two generations of the Moreton family, principally through the 16th century, ending *c*.1610. Architecturally extravagant, it uses tried-and-tested timber-framing skills, ignoring order and balance, but fully exploiting the decorative possibilities of timber framing. Architectural historian Nicholas Cooper observes that 'each addition crashes into its predecessor without regard for symmetry or even for structural logic'.

Set in a courtyard plan, it is jettied, often coved out, with intricate, black-timber carving and structural framing, and wattle and daub infill painted white beneath pitched stone-tiled roofs. While the timber framing draws on medieval traditions, the detailed carving incorporates stylised traditional and Renaissance motifs. The chevron, quatrefoil and cusped lozenge infill on the panelling is striking (overleaf). Each section of the building appears to vie for attention.

The three-storey south range (*c*.1560–2), incorporating the gatehouse and elevated long gallery (opposite), is particularly powerful. The undulating ridgeline and windows beneath illustrate the distorted beauty of working in green structural timber. Aside from the south porch, which has a strong visual impact when approaching the hall, much of the power is retained within the inner court, where two magnificent polygonal bays of 1559 project themselves forward, looking into the cobbled yard.

The Great Hall (*c*.1504–8) and east range are the earliest phases, with the hall originally open but later modernised with the insertion of a floor in 1559. In the Parlour of the east range, the wall paintings are a particularly exciting glimpse into decoration in the 16th century, with painted panelling and, above this, a sequence of paintings (*c*.1580) that tell the story of Susannah and the Elders. SR

**Little Moreton Hall, Cheshire** · Tudor house · *15th and 16th centuries · Timber frame with wattle and daub infill, brick, stone-tile roof · Gift, 1938*

# Avian accommodation

Willington Dovecote is one of the largest and most striking examples of a 16th-century dovecote in England. The dovecote and its neighbouring stable are the remains of a complex of manorial buildings, built between 1535 and 1541, possibly reusing stone from Newnham Priory, which was dissolved in 1535. Their creator was Sir John Gostwick (d.1545), Master of the Horse to Cardinal Wolsey (1470/1–1530) and later Treasurer and Receiver-General to Henry VIII (1491–1547).

Built of limestone rubble with ashlar dressings and a red clay-tile roof, pronounced corbelled crow-stepped gables give the building a dramatic outline against the sky. A series of louvres elevate the roofline, like a pagoda rising from the English countryside. Inside, the structure is no less startling, with nesting boxes accommodating up to 1,500 birds.

During the Tudor period, pigeon was considered a luxury food. Of course, one cannot control where pigeons feed, and inevitably they will feast on the grain in surrounding fields. This could lead to a landlord taking additional 'payment' from his tenants, since their grain was fattening his birds. EG

**Willington Dovecote, Bedfordshire** · Tudor dovecote ·
*Mid-16th century · Limestone, clay-tile roof · Gift, 1914*

# More window than wall

Without doubt one of the architectural mega-stars of the National Trust, Hardwick Hall is like a glittering galleon atop its hill, more window than wall. Its creator, Elizabeth Hardwick (?1527–1608), married four times, acquiring further nobility and wealth each time. By the time she died, Bess of Hardwick – as she was better known – was one of the country's richest and most powerful women. Children from her second marriage founded the Cavendish dynasty that built Chatsworth, while her fourth marriage, to George Talbot, made her Countess of Shrewsbury.

Bess turned to one of the earliest well-known architects, Robert Smythson, and what he created for her is comparable to his nearby masterpiece at Wollaton Hall (1580–8). The proportions of the house, its tall, narrow windows and four-storey towers accentuating the verticality of the elevations, draw the eye upwards. The roofline is laced with Bess's ES style, her countess's coronet, and the Cavendish coat of arms, supported by the Hardwick stags. These devices recur throughout the house in the ornate plasterwork of the Great Hall and Little Withdrawing Room overmantels and the majestic frieze of the High Great Chamber, a 1.8-metre-high forest scene featuring boar-

hunting and the goddess Diana. Such themes from Classical antiquity are characteristic of the early Renaissance.

Marble, black-stone and alabaster are crisply carved in chimneypieces, doorcases and panelling. The Long Gallery has two fireplaces, one with an overmantel featuring Mercy, the other shows Justice elevated on a pedestal, framed within scrolls and strapwork, between paired pilasters. The exquisite quality of design and carving are exemplified in the chimneypiece of the High Great Chamber and the doorcase of the Green Velvet Room.

The internal plan borrows from its medieval ancestors only in the adherence to the convention of the double-height Great Hall. However, this hall is entered end-on, with the stone and plasterwork screen adding a sense of drama as the room opens up. The hall is flanked by pantry, serving (surveying) room and buttery, with the first floor largely given over to chambers. The highest-status rooms are elevated on the second floor: the magnificent Long Gallery, now hung with tapestries, paintings and punctuated by the lavish canopy, and the High Great Chamber.

This house is of exceptional quality, and survives remarkably intact inside and out, along with a dazzling collection dating from the 16th century. EG

**Hardwick Hall, Derbyshire** · Elizabethan mansion · *Robert Smythson (c.1535–1614)* · *1590s* · *Sandstone, lead roofs* · *National Land Fund, 1959*

*Far left* · Elizabeth Hardwick, later Talbot ('Bess of Hardwick'), Countess of Shrewsbury, in a portrait of *c.*1560 at Hardwick Hall by a follower of Hans Eworth (NT 1129165).
*Left* · Marble decoration and panelling in Hardwick's Green Velvet Room.

# Miniature mansion

Montacute House was built at the turn of the 17th century by Sir Edward Phelips (c.1560–1614). He was a lawyer and member of parliament, holding offices including Speaker of the House of Commons and Master of the Rolls. He opened for the prosecution at the trial of Guy Fawkes and in 1610 became Chancellor of the Duchy of Cornwall. Phelips was an ambitious man and he needed a house to match, so he turned to local architect William Arnold.

Early visitors to Montacute would have approached the house via the East Courtyard, entering beneath a gatehouse, now lost. The two pavilions at either corner (overleaf) were designed as lodgings for guests, perfect miniature mansions with exquisite detailing. Their outlines bristle with pinnacles, ogee roofs topped with openwork ball finials, a corbelled, moulded parapet and transomed and mullioned bay windows.

They originally had two floors and were furnished with fireplaces to warm their guests. The chimneys are shown in an early 19th-century watercolour by John Buckler but were removed by Lord Curzon during his 'restoration' post-1915. EG

**Montacute House, Somerset** · Elizabethan pavilion ·
*William Arnold (d.1636–7) · c.1601 · Ham Hill limestone,
slate roof · Gift through SPAB, 1931*

*Above* · Sir Edward Phelips in a late 18th-century painting by an unknown artist, copied from an earlier original (NT 597909). The Speaker's mace and bag of office can be seen beneath the window.

# Founded on faith

A roofless shell, Lyveden was begun in 1596 for Thomas Tresham (1543–1605), and has been attributed to Robert Stickells, Clerk of Works at Richmond Palace, although no drawings survive. Never completed, it was built as a summerhouse for banqueting and entertaining. The crisp limestone structure rises like a winged spaceship from its emerald-green platform. It stands two storeys above ground with an undercroft, and is cruciform in plan, with a projecting octagonal bay at the end of each wing.

This enigmatic building speaks of a time when religion divided society. Holding the 'wrong' beliefs often brought exclusion and persecution, and could lead to imprisonment or even death.

Thomas Tresham created a spiritual landscape and, within it, a grand building quietly expressive of deeply held conviction. The frieze above the ground-floor windows is carved with symbols of his Catholic faith, including instruments of the passion and Judas's money bag, and the upper frieze is inscribed *Jesus mundi Salus – Gaude Mater Virgo Maria* (Jesus the world's salvation – Rejoice, Mary, Virgin mother). EG

**Lyveden New Bield, Northamptonshire** · Banqueting house · *Attributed to Robert Stickells (d.1620)* · *c.1604–5* · *Ashlar with white limestone dressings* · *Purchased by subscription, 1922*

## Bold Jacobean

Built around the bones of Nicholas Dagworth's moated house of 1390, Blickling is a boldly Jacobean mansion, created between 1619 and 1628 by architect Robert Lyminge, one of only a handful of known architects of the period. It was built for Sir Henry Hobart (*c*.1554–1625), a member of parliament and a highly successful lawyer.

The original plan was a double courtyard, with the Great Hall arranged, medieval-style, across the 'belt', separating the southerly Little Court from the Long Court beyond. Little Court held the formal spaces, including the south-facing Withdrawing Chamber, Chapel, Parlour and Great Staircase. The second, northern courtyard – Long Court – was surrounded by lodgings and service spaces. The Long Gallery, which also accommodates the magnificent Library, runs along the east range.

Blickling is built of red brick with stone and stucco dressings. The principal, south front is largely symmetrical and has seven bays with projecting window bays, strapwork and Classical ornament. Ogee-topped four-storey turrets mark each corner. The flanking wings, with their handsome Dutch gables, are contemporary with the main house and contained stables and further service accommodation.

Blickling exemplifies Jacobean style. The main entrance is flanked by Doric columns and ornamented with Hobart's heraldic bulls, female figures and swags. It supports the 12-light first-floor window above, complete with Ionic pilasters and figures of Justice and Truth. Internally, the star of the show is undoubtedly the plasterwork, carried out by Edward Stanyon (1581–*c*.1632). It reaches its zenith in the 38-metre Long Gallery (opposite), where panels of Hobart arms and symbols of the five senses and learning alternate down the centre. Panels to either side are copied from plates in Henry Peacham's *Minerva Britanna, or, A Garden of Heroical Devises* (1612). EG

**Blickling Hall, Norfolk** · Jacobean mansion · *Robert Lyminge (active 1607–28)* · *c.1616* · *Red brick with stone and stucco dressings, plain and pantile roofs with lead domes to corner turrets* · *Acquired under the will of the 11th Marquess of Lothian, 1942*

*Right* · Sir Henry Hobart (*c*.1554–1625), the 'builder of Blickling', in a portrait of 1616 by an unknown artist in the circle of William Larkin (*c*.1585–1619) (NT 357150).

# Unique survivor

This little gem of a building is a unique survivor of a once-popular pastime, the coursing of deer by greyhounds. The activity is now illegal, but the purpose was to pitch the speed of greyhounds against that of deer – a spectator sport with a strong betting tradition attached.

Built around 1634 for John Dutton (1594–1657) of Sherborne House, Lodge Park shows the influence of Palladianism. The front elevation is of five bays with tall mullioned and transomed windows. The *piano nobile* windows are topped with broken pediments 'clasping' busts and simple strapwork ornament, with balustrade above. Entrance is through an arcaded porch with deeply rusticated columns. It is arranged across three floors, with a kitchen and service rooms in the basement, a large entrance hall and further service rooms at ground level, and a banqueting hall with viewing balcony at first-floor level. There is also a viewing platform on the roof.

The elegant proportion and refined use of architectural detailing have led to comparisons with Inigo Jones's Whitehall Banqueting House, built in 1607. The architect of Lodge Park is not known for certain, but the most likely possibility is that the design was by Balthazar Gerbier (1592–1663), who was working in the area, and that it was executed by local architect Valentine Strong (d.1662), who enlarged Sherborne House for John Dutton in 1651–3. EG

**Lodge Park, Gloucestershire** · Deer-coursing grandstand · *Architect uncertain · c.1634 · Limestone ashlar, lead roof · 7th Baron Sherborne bequest, 1987*

*Right* · The coursing of fallow deer depicted in an etching of c.1671, after Francis Barlow (1622–1704).

# Noble gatekeeper

Lanhydrock's gatehouse is the fittingly splendid portal into the walled entrance courtyard of what was a fine 17th-century house, set amid a designed landscape in which the gatehouse was the main eyecatcher. Demolition works in 1780 and a catastrophic fire in 1881 saw large parts of the house destroyed. However, some portions, including the magnificent Long Gallery in the north range and the gatehouse, survived.

Built by John and Lucy Robartes, commemorated in a datestone 'ILR1651', the gatehouse is rectangular in plan with an octagonal tower at either end, giving it a floorplan rather akin to a pair of binoculars. The tower to the right has a guard room at ground-floor level and small unheated chamber above. The tower to the left contains the stair and closets. At first-floor level there is a heated central chamber, whose chimney stack is concealed within the parapet. The striking, crow-stepped parapet is surmounted by disproportionately tall obelisks, giving its roofline the appearance of wearing a spiky, baubled crown. EG

**Lanhydrock, Cornwall** · Jacobean gatehouse ·
*c.1651 · Granite ashlar, lead roof · Gift, 1953*

# Vernacular charm

Sometimes a building type evolves that is so supremely suited to its environment that it becomes emblematic of that locality. The Cumbrian bank barn is just such a building. It is a multi-purpose structure, so much more than just a barn, providing for the wide-ranging farming needs of a steeply sloping upland environment. The example at Townend is also rather beautiful.

One feature that adds to this aesthetic charm is the 'spinning gallery', which flanks the ramped threshing bay entrance and overhangs the animal housing below. Narrow ventilation slits show where grain and straw are stored. Two wings project either side of the main barn range, creating a sheltered area in the embrace of the building, staving off the rain and providing dry storage and a protected workspace.

The embodiment of vernacular architecture, the Townend barn has grown from the stone beneath its feet, been roofed with slates from a nearby field quarry, and crafted by local builders using skills learned and perfected in the same valley and passed down over generations. It is dated 1666 and, as is often the case with farm buildings, has been added to and adapted over the centuries. EG

**Townend, Cumbria** · Bank barn · *1666* · *Limewashed rubble stone, diminished-course slate roof · Gift, 1948*

# Hold your horses

William Morgan (c.1640–80) attached great importance to his equestrian skills, perceiving them as an expression of his status and masculinity, and the magnificent stables he built demonstrate this eloquently.

Tredegar's stables and riding school are contemporary with the great Restoration rebuild of the house, c.1664–72. The complex includes grooms' quarters, tack and feed rooms. Unusually, the range of buildings is at the front of the house, forming one side of an open courtyard. This further demonstrates the importance to Morgan of his horses.

A pediment with a clock straddles the three central bays, with projecting 'pavilions' terminating either end. The entrance passage has an elaborate broken pediment clasping a Classical Roman bust. Two suits of armour, cannons and drums are arranged above the pediment, which sits astride a pair of Corinthian pilasters. Ten mullion and transom windows, with oval *oeuil-de-boeuf* openings above, are interspersed with three-quarter-height Ionic pilasters, each crowned with cupped acorn finials. EG

**Tredegar House, Newport** · Restoration house ·
*c.1664–72 · Red brick, slate roof · Long lease from
Newport Council since 2012*

# Phases of history

The 'Plantation of Ulster', which began during the 1610s, saw the confiscation of lands from Irish Catholic families and their transfer into the hands of incoming English-speaking Protestants, principally from the north of England and the Scottish Lowlands. The Springhill lands were conveyed to one such plantation family, the Conynghams of Ayrshire, in around 1658.

The first reference to the present house is a marriage settlement of 1680, wherein William Conyngham undertakes to 'erect a convenient dwelling house of lime and stone, two stories high, with necessary office houses, gardens and orchards'. Tree-ring dating indicates a building programme in the 1690s. The resulting house is remarkable for the survival of many of its surrounding service courtyards and outbuildings, the style and manner of building reflecting the family's Scottish roots. The two single-storey flanking wings were added to the house from the later 18th century, when the pavilions – originally the stables and brewhouse – were enhanced with elegant details such as pointed Gothic-style windows. EG

**Springhill, County Londonderry** · Plantation house · *c.1697 · Rendered rubble masonry, slate roof · Gift, 1957*

# Towering terraces

The 17th century saw prolonged religious tension, which exploded into decades of civil war and revolution. The Earls of Powis were devout Catholics and supporters of the Stuart monarchy, and were deeply enmeshed in the turbulence.

However, between periods of imprisonment in the Tower of London and exile in France, William Herbert, 3rd Baron Powis (c.1626–96), 1st Earl, Marquess and titular Duke, carried out considerable improvements to his castle. He created a state apartment to rival that of the King and then began work creating one of the finest Baroque Italian terraced gardens in Europe.

Possibly designed by William Winde, who had created the Grand Staircase (overleaf) during the 1670s, Powis's magnificent terracing is a rare survivor of Baroque bravado. Staggeringly steep, cleverly taking advantage of the red sandstone outcrop on which the castle is built, the cascading arcades, draped with vibrant blooms and topped with ancient yews, are among Powis's great symbols of status.

The towering terraces are built of red sandstone and red brick, with pale sandstone quoins, dressings and balustrades. The Orangery is of seven bays, with tall sash windows. The central three bays are advanced and the central

doorway is flanked by pilasters supporting a moulded entablature. The segmental arch is of lightly rusticated stone and the tympanum is filled with ornamental ironwork. A stone cornice runs above, with balustrading punctuated by plinths supporting leadwork statuary by Dutch sculptor John Nost II (d.1729).

The next tier holds the Aviary, an open arcade with balustrade above, this time ornamented with lead urns. The top tier resembles a garden picture gallery in which pedimented niches house resplendent flower-filled urns. Lace-like balustrading and vast clipped yews form the top frame. Beyond the Orangery, Aviary and 'picture gallery', the terraces stretch their arms wide, and are planted with espaliered fruit trees and billowing herbaceous borders.

To the east front of the castle is a single high terrace, abutting the grand stepped approach. When built, it was topped with a banqueting house that overlooked further formal compartmented gardens, now lost to 18th-century landscaping. The eastern flank of the terrace terminates in magnificent gilded gates, which were installed in celebration of Lord Powis's elevation to Marquess and titular Duke. EG

**Powis Castle, Powys** · Baroque terraced garden ·
*Attributed to William Winde (c.1642–1722) · late 17th century*
*· Red brick and sandstone · National Land Fund, 1965*

## Windswept in Wales

The majority of buildings in the care of the National Trust are best described as vernacular. They are cottages, field barns and farmsteads, and they pepper our rural landscapes. Built from local stone, timber and earth in styles adapted to their localities, they tell of past ways of life.

Treleddyd Fawr is a former farmhouse, built from rubble stone, with a slate roof. The Pembrokeshire landscape is exposed to the prevailing wet south-westerly winds, so the whole building is coated in layers of limewash to repel the brutal weather. This extends to the roof, where its application is known as slobbering.

The tiny windows are positioned to provide light precisely where needed, not to create a consciously balanced façade. Draft-exclusion measures include a deep porch, internal timber 'wind-partition' and a high-backed settle.

The house is surrounded – or to borrow an evocative Welsh word, *cwtched* (hugged) – by the other farmstead buildings, small structures huddled around a yard. Differently sized doors hint at their various uses: cowshed, hayloft and granary, pigsties, stable and cart-shed. EG

**Treleddyd Fawr, Pembrokeshire** · Farmhouse · *Early 18th century* · *Stone, slate roof, limewash* · *Glyn Griffiths bequest, 2013*

# International connections

In 1686 government administrator William Blathwayt (c.1649–1717) married Mary Wynter (1650–91), with intentions for her ancestral estate clear from the start: 'I am afraid there will be a necessity of building a new house at Dirham …'. Between 1692 and 1704 all was replaced in a fashionable Baroque style.

A little-known Huguenot, Samuel Hauduroy, designed the west front (right) and probably provided the interior paint-effect schemes, replicating walnut, Prince's-Wood and marble. The refined east front (overleaf) was by architect William Talman, Comptroller of the Royal Works, with his crown colleague George London (c.1640–1714) helping to lay out the ambitious gardens.

Dyrham embodied Blathwayt's multiple professional interests. His career started in The Netherlands and peaked under King William III (1650–1702) – Dutch connections reflected in Delftware and gilt leather wall hangings. From his tenure as Secretary at War, abroad in Flanders throughout the house's construction, derive military manuals and paintings of fortifications. Blathwayt was also the government's most significant colonial administrator, articulated through imported timbers from Virginia and Carolina, and the display of exotic plants, such as sizeable aloes guarding the Greenhouse door.

In 1717 Colen Campbell published the second volume of *Vitruvius Britannicus*, which featured Dyrham's east elevation and floorplan, stating: 'the learned Patron has spared no Expense in leaving such lasting monuments of his Liberality'. Dyrham is not simply an indulgence afforded by wealth, but a statement about Blathwayt's professional status, which has left a material record for an age of colonialism, conflict, and economic and political revolution. RG

**Dyrham Park, Gloucestershire** · Baroque mansion · *Samuel Hauduroy (active c.1690–c.1700) and William Talman (c.1650–1719) · 1692–1704 · Limestone ashlar, slate and lead roof · National Land Fund, 1956*

*Below* · Dyrham's east front, as illustrated in Volume II of Colen Campbell's *Vitruvius Britannicus* (1717, plate 91).

# Vanbrugh's last great house

The architecture of Sir John Vanbrugh is enormously distinctive. He had a style that embraced Palladian ideas, referenced Elizabethan grandeur, stirred in a hefty slug of Scottish Baronial solidity, and turned up the volume on texture and shade. This is exciting architecture and provided this Protestant poet and former playwright with a second career, into which he threw himself with characteristic passion.

Seaton Delaval Hall, built between *c.*1718 and 1728 for Admiral George Delaval (1668–1723), is Vanbrugh's last great house, making it the youngest sibling of the architectural giants Blenheim Palace and Castle Howard. Featuring a heavily textured façade, strong shadow lines give a sense of depth, and with characteristic Vanbrugh rusticated basement, quoins and columns, it might well be described as 'muscle architecture'.

This is late English Baroque at its finest. A majestic central block houses principal rooms, with loggias connecting to two long, narrow service wings, facing onto the grand court. The theme of strong rustication continues along the wings, and the whole roofline is punctuated with finials, urns and pedestals that were intended to accommodate Classical figures. The statues appear in Colen Campbell's elevation drawing

in *Vitruvius Britannicus* (1715–25) but were never added to the building.

Today, the house feels filled with optimism and light. However, the story of Seaton Delaval Hall took a tragic turn on the night of 3 January 1822, when a fire consumed the interior of the principal block and the south-east wing. It remained roofless and derelict until *c*.1862, when architect John Dobson installed a roof, but otherwise the building remained largely an uninhabited shell, with the family later creating an apartment in the kitchen wing.

Recently conserved stucco figures representing architecture, painting, music, sculpture and geography gaze down on the Entrance Hall. Marble and limestone floors have also been restored, along with Classical figures and low-relief panels decorating the fireplaces of these great rooms, which still bear the scars of the fire two centuries ago. EG

**Seaton Delaval Hall, Northumberland** · Late Baroque mansion · *Sir John Vanbrugh (1664–1726)* · *c*.1718–28 · *Sandstone ashlar, Lakeland slate and lead roofs* · *Accepted in lieu of inheritance tax, and public appeal, 2009*

*Right* · Sir John Vanbrugh (1664–1726) in a portrait of *c*.1705 by Sir Godfrey Kneller (1646–1723).

# Gently tread the cave

The 18th century witnessed advances in many areas. Science, philosophy and the arts were discussed in fashionable coffee shops and salons, and the sons of the wealthy embarked on the grand tour, travelling around continental Europe, often with a tutor, to experience its culture, history and scenery. They returned awash with the literature, art and architecture of Classical Europe, and of Italy in particular, and a desire to recreate Classical landscapes in the parklands around their grand houses. Here, idyll, art and architecture became intertwined.

In 1725 Stourhead house was completed by architect Colen Campbell (1676–1729) for Henry Hoare I (1677–1725) in Palladian style. His son, Henry Hoare II (known as 'Henry the Magnificent', 1705–85), created the landscape gradually from 1744 onwards. The great set piece at its heart is comprised of the Pantheon (1753–62), lake (1754–5) and Palladian Bridge (c.1762). The Grotto was extended in 1776 with the addition of the passage.

From the central vaulted chamber a passage leads to the River God's cave, which houses a statue by John Cheere (1709–87). A nymph reclines in an arched recess off the main chamber, accompanied by Alexander Pope's lines, incised in the pool's marble edging (right).

The elegant style of the lettering was used as a basis for the National Trust typeface.

The Grotto has a brick structure clad in rugged sponge stone with a decorative cobbled floor. It creates the illusion of having been carved out by an underground torrent, leaving behind a space for quiet contemplation. EG

**Stourhead, Wiltshire** · Grotto · *William Privet of Chilmark (dates unknown)* · *1748 and 1776* · *Brick and sponge stone* · *Gift, 1946–7*

# Triumphant focal point

In the mid-1720s Bath stone entrepreneur Ralph Allen (c.1693–1764) met member of parliament and landowner Robert Gay (c.1676–1738) and architect John Wood the Elder (1704–54). This encounter led to the transformation of Bath into the 'it' place for polite society to congregate and take the waters.

Between 1726 and 1728, Allen purchased land on the north edge of Bath. He commissioned designs for a new house from Wood the Elder and Prior Park was built between c.1733 and c.1750.

Between 1734 and c.1740, with advice from Alexander Pope (1688–1744), Allen began to populate Prior Park's landscape, adding a grotto, a serpentine river and a wilderness garden. The triumphant focal point is Richard Jones's Palladian bridge, introduced during the 1750s to span the cascade. It was copied from Roger Morris's bridge at Wilton, which was built only a year before James Gibbs's Palladian bridge at Stowe. All three are modelled on a rejected design of c.1556 for the Rialto Bridge in Venice by Andrea Palladio (1508–80). EG

**Prior Park Landscape Garden, Somerset** · Palladian bridge · *Richard Jones (dates unknown)* · *1750s* · *Bath stone ashlar, slate roof* · *Gift, 1993*

# Neo-classical grandeur

In 1759, following the death of his father, Nathaniel Curzon (1726–1804), 1st Baron Scarsdale, began a programme of transformation at his family home, Kedleston Hall. It was to become one of the finest Neo-classical houses in England.

The new Kedleston Hall was a shamelessly grand architectural statement. Curzon chose a design by architect Matthew Brettingham, who had taken his inspiration from Palladio's Villa Mocenigo, illustrated in Book II of Palladio's *Il Quattro Libri dell'Architettura* (1570). The villa has a central block with quadrant colonnades linking to four pavilions. In plan, it has the appearance of a squashed frog. However, only the two northerly legs were executed.

Much of the work to rebuild Kedleston was supervised by architect James Paine, who had collaborated with Robert Adam at Nostell Priory. Had the full intended plan been completed at both houses, they would have appeared remarkably similar, but Kedleston's character is much livelier, with depth and animation to its façades.

Seemingly attracting great architects into his orbit, Curzon had commissioned Adam to create a landscape at Kedleston and to design garden buildings, including north and south lodges, bath-house, boathouse, an elegant three-arch

bridge and an orangery. When consulted, Adam suggested changes to Brettingham's designs and by 1760 Curzon had placed him fully in charge of the project.

Brettingham, Paine and Adam were all inspired by the architecture of Andrea Palladio but chose to use the ingredients in different ways. The result is a house of two different characters. It bears one somewhat predictable elevation: the north side – wide, winged, with Corinthian columns supporting the obligatory portico and statuary above a rusticated basement. Its opposite, south face is embracing, curvaceous and celebratory, with Adam's dome crowning the Saloon rotunda clearly visible. The Corinthian order is continued, but this time with detached columns, each supporting its own chunk of deep entablature.

Internally, the Saloon is clearly inspired by the Pantheon in Rome, with successive impressive interiors painted and carved with scenes from antiquity, all to Adam's designs. The finest space, however, is the Marble Hall, with its pink alabaster columns, refined plasterwork and grisaille panels. Kedleston is the perfect study in Neo-classical design. EG

**Kedleston Hall, Derbyshire** · Palladian mansion · *Principally Robert Adam (1728–92), with Matthew Brettingham (1699 1769) and James Paine (c.1717 89) · 1759 65 · Red brick with ashlar and render, Welsh slate roof · Gift, 1987*

# Pyramid scheme

The Augustinian priory that gave Nostell its name was lost to the Dissolution of the Monasteries in 1540 and soon afterwards the surviving monastic buildings were converted into a house. The site was bought in 1654 by the Winn family, whose fortune had been made in the textile trade. Three generations later, and having benefitted from generous marriage settlements, Sir Rowland Winn (1706–65), 4th Baronet, commissioned amateur architect Colonel James Moyser (c.1688–1751) to design a magnificent new Palladian mansion. James Paine (c.1717–89) then adapted these designs, creating a central block with four connected pavilions at each corner. The 5th Baronet, also Sir Rowland Winn, brought in the hugely fashionable Robert Adam to update the plans, creating additional interiors and populating the park with pavilions and lodges.

Situated to the north of the house and straddling the north drive, one of these pavilions, the Obelisk Lodge, was constructed to an Adam design in 1776 or 1777 and was originally known as Featherstone Lodge. Its striking form is that of a narrow pyramid – or rather squat obelisk – with a flatter pyramidal tip. The building feels almost alien, as though a giant bird had dropped it on top of an unsuspecting little Tuscan temple.

The lodge's sandstone faces are smooth and largely unornamented save for the gaping archway framed with massive Tuscan columns and pedimented entablature. A cornice runs around the pyramid from the pediment and there is a blind circular window above it. The lodge sits astride a short length of park wall. Small rooms at ground- and first-floor levels are lit by narrow windows and warmed by fires whose chimneys rise within the pyramid. It must have provided a curious sight to visitors arriving on a winter's night, with windows glowing like golden eyes and smoke rising from the apex of the pyramid. EG

**Nostell, West Yorkshire** · Neo-classical lodge · *Design by Robert Adam (1728–92) · 1776–7 · Sandstone ashlar · Purchased with HLF funds, 2002*

# Georgian townhouse

Liverpool's commercial success in transatlantic trading through the 18th and 19th centuries saw rapid and massive redevelopment. By 1740, Liverpool was Europe's largest trader in enslaved people, with ships returning to Liverpool laden with tobacco, sugar, rum and cotton. This huge influx of money was translated into smart townhouses and public architecture, a relationship that was starkly exposed by the Reverend William Bagshaw Stevens in 1797 when he described the city as a 'large built Town' where 'every Brick is cemented to its fellow brick by the blood and sweat' of enslaved people.

Rodney Street was laid out by William Roscoe and others on the eastern fringe of the town in 1783–4 and evolved piecemeal up to the 1820s. Despite this, there is a clear intention to create the illusion of cohesion by the use of a pediment over the five-bay house, suggesting something grander than a series of modest homes.

Georgian townhouses are typified by tall sash windows and a smart front door with a fanlight. Wrought iron was used for ornament such as railings, balconies and lantern brackets, and the detailing is largely Neo-classical in character. EG

**59 Rodney Street, Liverpool** · Georgian terrace · *1783–4 · Red brick with rendered dressings, Welsh slate roof · Edward Chambré Hardman Trust Gift, 2002*

# In the round

Passion can lead to many things: intense emotional connection, creativity or tragedy. Mussenden Temple, perched on the edge of a cliff overlooking the wild Atlantic, embodies all these: the passion of the fanciful Frederick Hervey, Earl Bishop of Derry (1730–1803), for circular Classical buildings, for the wildness of the Londonderry coastline and for his beautiful cousin Frideswide Mussenden, who died tragically young at the age of 22.

The younger son of the Hervey family, Frederick entered the Church with no great hopes for the future, but through a mixture of luck, force of personality and the untimely death of his two older brothers, he attained the Bishopric of Derry, one of the richest in Ireland, and succeeded to the family title as 4th Earl of Bristol. Never one to spend too much time devoted to his flock, his later years were dedicated to Italy, collecting antique sculpture and inspiration for his architectural projects. His first circular house, at Ballyscullion, no longer survives, and his oval house at Ickworth, Suffolk (pages 116–17), was left unfinished at his death, but Mussenden Temple, the first and most dramatic of his creations, has survived, although the interior finishes are lost.

Inspired by Classical and Renaissance architecture, it is an elegantly simple structure: above the crypt is a large, circular chamber, which housed the Earl Bishop's library beneath a coffered dome, with ocean views to the north, east and west. The dome is topped by a large Classical urn and the massive stone drum is adorned with 16 attached Corinthian columns, holding up an entablature decorated with bishops' mitres and the Earl's heraldic 'ounces' (spotted leopards) along with a stirring text from Lucretius's *De Rerum Natura*, which Dryden translated as: 'Tis pleasant, safely to behold from shore / The rolling ship, and hear the tempest roar'. FB

**Mussenden Temple, Downhill, County Londonderry**
· Neo-classical rotunda library · *Michael Shanahan (1731–1811)* · *1783–5* · *Limestone, copper roof* · *Gift, 1949*

## Industrial microcosm

The Industrial Revolution of the late 18th century transformed the landscape, urban and rural, and altered for ever the position of Britain on the global trade map.

Samuel Greg (1758–1834) was one of the entrepreneurs who embraced the new technologies and demand for goods, building his first mill in 1784 and doubling it in size in 1796. In 1797 Greg built his family home next to the mill and developed Styal village for his employees. The completeness of the community makes Quarry Bank and Styal a remarkable survival.

Raw cotton was transported via the Bridgewater Canal from Liverpool. Initially powered by the River Bollin running through its valley, and later by massive steam engines, Quarry Bank Mill grew to become one of the largest cotton-manufacturing businesses in the world.

The earliest, three-bay portion of the mill has a stone-coped pediment with a clock and a bell cupola to its roof, along with an inscription reading 'Quarry Bank Mills Built by Samuel Greg Esquire of Belfast Ireland Anno Domini 1784'. This diminutive structure was quickly extended through the early 19th century, with a second water wheel (10m in diameter) added in 1819.

In 1810 the first steam engine, by Boulton and Watt, had been bought to supplement dwindling summertime river flow, and a huge octagonal chimney was added. When Greg's son Robert took over in 1834, he added the four-storey weaving shed with 305 looms, which required its extensive floors, laden with iron machinery, to be supported by iron columns.

Styal village was developed around a clutch of older farms and cottages to serve the new mill community. It combines terraces and cottages of different sizes, such as Oak Cottages (opposite), each having their own allotment and privy. All are built of red brick and Welsh slate with cast-iron small-pane or timber-sash windows and stone steps and cobbles. The community was served by school, shops and chapels – one Methodist, converted from a seed store, and Norcliffe Baptist Chapel, built by Samuel Greg in 1823 in a Gothic style with timber-framed porch and bellcote.

Greg also built the apprentices' house by the road between the mill and Styal village in 1790. It is rectangular in plan, brick-built, with a roof of two parallel ridges, three storeys high. It accommodated up to 90 children, aged as young as eight, who were put to work in the mill. Nine years later he added Quarry Bank House, a modest Georgian villa with a projecting central bay, in rendered brick with a glass-roofed porch on fluted columns in a nod to Neo-classical nicety.

Unlike other successful industrialists, Greg chose to live on site, in the midst of mill life, his family home and garden built to overlook the Bollin that provided the energy to power his empire. EG

**Quarry Bank Mill and Styal Village, Cheshire** · Cotton mill, terraced cottages, apprentices' accommodation and Georgian villa · *1784 onwards (mill), 1790 (apprentices' house), 1797 (Quarry Bank House), 1820 (Styal cottages)* · *Red brick (Quarry Bank House), Welsh slate roof* · Greg Gift, 1939 (Mill and Estate); purchase, 2006 (Quarry Bank House, Lower Garden); purchase, 2010 (Upper Garden)

# Dining in style

The 18th century witnessed an obsession with the Classical world. This was the era of the grand tour, from which architects, artists and wealthy patrons returned laden with sketches of Greek and Roman ruins, pictures and sculpture to adorn their modern temples.

One of the finest is the Temple of the Winds at Mount Stewart, designed by James 'Athenian' Stuart for the 1st Marquess of Londonderry. The temple is inspired by the Tower of the Winds in Athens, an octagonal building dating from at least 50BC. It has a frieze carved with the eight winds, hence the name, and each face also has a sundial. Stuart reinterpreted this at Mount Stewart as a banqueting house, set on a small hill overlooking Strangford Lough with the Mourne Mountains in the distance.

Two of the eight faces have small porticoes raised on fluted columns of a restrained Corinthian order, which support viewing balconies. At the rear is a domed, cylindrical turret housing a spiral staircase. Internally, the space is exquisitely decorated, with marquetry floor by John Ferguson, who also worked on the main house, and low-relief plasterwork ceiling by William Fitzgerald of Dublin. EG

**Temple of the Winds, Mount Stewart, County Down** · Neo-classical banqueting house · *James 'Athenian' Stuart (1713–88) · 1785 · Scrabo sandstone facing, slate roof · Lady Mairi Bury Gift, 1962*

# Sacred to the memory

The Templetown Mausoleum was designed by the great Neo-classical architect Robert Adam in one of his rare appearances on Irish soil. Adam had been commissioned in the 1780s by Clotworthy Upton, 1st Baron Templetown (1721–85), to carry out alterations to his house, Castle Upton, and it appears that his sister-in-law Sarah Upton took advantage of Adam's involvement to commission a mausoleum for her late husband the Rt Hon. Arthur Upton (1715–68), Clotworthy's elder brother. It was completed in 1789.

Built of pale-grey limestone, the mausoleum is not excessively embellished – other than a cornice with dentil course and plain frieze, the decoration is concentrated on the entrance front. Two Coadestone roundels with shallow-relief figures and a pair of urns occupy niches either side of the arched entry, with a third on a plinth above it. The plinth is decorated with swags and a foliated roundel above a marble tablet declaring, 'Sacred to the Memory of the Right Honourable Arthur Upton'. EG

**Templetown Mausoleum, County Antrim** · Neo-classical mausoleum · *Robert Adam (1728–92)* · *1789* · *Limestone ashlar and rubble stone, limestone ashlar pyramidal roof* · *Gift, 1964*

*Above* · Robert Adam (1728–92) in a portrait of *c.*1770–4 attributed to George Willison (1741–97).

# Hooked on classics

Ickworth is the product of a passion for rotundas. The creation of Frederick Hervey (1730–1803), Bishop of Derry, and 4th Earl of Bristol, it follows his now lost house, built 1787 at Ballyscullion, also a crescent with central rotunda, and the gloriously located Mussenden Temple (pages 106–7), a small rotund library perched high on the cliffs of Downhill, County Londonderry. He spent a great deal of time in Italy, where his obsession with this Classical form clearly took hold.

An avid collector, in 1781 he commissioned Mario Asprucci to design a setting for the display of his collection at Ickworth. This was implemented in 1795 by Francis Sandys, who had worked for the Earl Bishop in Ireland. The Rotunda has two tiers of pilasters, Ionic below, with Corinthian above, topped by a terracotta frieze with a second frieze running between the Ionic register. These were created by the Carabelli brothers of Milan, and are based on John Flaxman's drawings of episodes from Homeric literature (below).

It was intended that the Rotunda should be fitted out as a family home and the flanking wings set out to display his growing collection of art but in 1798 Hervey's art collection was confiscated by Napoleonic troops. He spent his remaining years, until his death in 1803, campaigning for the return of the collection and did not see the building completed. EG

**Ickworth, Suffolk** · Neo-classical mansion · *Mario Asprucci (1764–1804)* · *1795 onwards* · *Stuccoed brick, slate and lead roofs* · *National Land Fund, 1956*

# High-risk roofing

The long, narrow settlement of Branscombe, centred on a Norman church and meandering down to the seashore, has evolved over the centuries. Early and later buildings mingle, many united by their thatched roofs, including the 18th-century village forge. Perhaps an unlikely choice of material for a forge, its thatched roof is like a great bonnet on this little building, dipping low to the ground, where it is extended to cover a sheltered area and a wood-store, supported on timber posts.

Typically for this part of Devon, the walls are of small, poor-quality rubble stone and thick lime mortar. The main room, or smithy, where the blacksmith works his craft, retains its 18th-century forge with a more recent brick chimney to safely convey smoke and sparks away. Village forges that produce ornamental ironwork – gates, railings and weathervanes – are a rarity today. Historically, however, little buildings like this one would have been at the heart of every community, in an age when the horse was the tractor that kept the country fed. EG

**Branscombe Forge, Devon** · Forge · *18th and 19th century* · *Rubble stone, thatch roof · National Land Fund, 1965*

# Agricultural archetype

Samuel Wyatt was commissioned *c.*1803 by Thomas, 1st Viscount Anson (1767–1818), to renovate Shugborough Hall. Wyatt was a keen exponent of Neo-classical architecture, having also been Clerk of Works to Robert Adam, with whom he worked on Kedleston Hall.

It is likely that Wyatt, a Lichfield local, was commissioned on the advice of Anson's wife, Lady Anne Coke of Holkham Hall, where, as estate architect, he had carried out large-scale agricultural improvements. Samuel Wyatt was employed by Anson to design two farmsteads, White Barn Farm and Park Farm, to serve a vast 2,000-acre farm.

Park Farm, designed as a showpiece, is what we refer to today as a model farm. The proliferation of 'organised' or 'model' farmstead design marked a shift from subsistence farming to larger-scale commercial farming, an agricultural revolution in tandem with the Industrial Revolution.

At Shugborough, White Barn Farm had one of the first water-driven threshing mills, while Park Farm had a water-powered cornmill. Two canals also border the estate, enabling excess produce – cheese, meat and livestock – to be exported to Birmingham, and fuel and lime to be transported to Shugborough in the large quantities required.

Built of red brick and slate, Park Farm is located in the centre of the park close to the Tower of the Winds, which Wyatt partially converted into a functioning dairy. The farmstead also includes a steward's house, stables, cattle-sheds, hoggery and a fowl house (left). EG

**Shugborough Park Farm, Staffordshire** · Model farm · *Samuel Wyatt (1737–1807) · c.1803 · Red brick, slate roof · National Land Fund, 1966*

# Blaise of glory

Thomas Farr was a transatlantic trader in goods and enslaved people. He built Blaise castle folly and pleasure grounds in 1766, reputedly in order to watch his ships returning to Bristol. In 1778 Farr became bankrupt after his ships were blockaded during the American War of Independence, and he sold the estate.

In 1789 Quaker banker John Scandrett Harford Sr (1754–1815) bought the Blaise estate. Harford commissioned Bristol architect William Paty to design a suitably chaste and plain home, and Blaise Castle House was duly completed in 1796. He then invited fashionable landscape architect Humphry Repton (1752–1818) to visit and Repton produced a Red Book for Blaise in 1796. This picturesque setting was to become the backdrop for Blaise Hamlet.

Harford commissioned John Nash, favourite architect of the Prince Regent, to build an ornamental dairy in c.1804 and an orangery in 1806. This can fairly be attributed to the encouragement of Repton, with whom Nash had entered into partnership. By 1810 Nash was creating a hamlet of nine individual *cottages ornés* as retirement homes for estate staff.

Each house in Blaise is different, evoking the organic nature of village evolution over centuries.

Materials and details combine the vernacular with the antiquarian. We see clustered diamond-set brick chimneys borrowed from Tudor times, thick stone-tile and thatched roofs (as shown in the 1867 archive photograph below), deeply overhanging eaves and pentices, small-paned windows and plain plank doors. EG

**Blaise Hamlet, Somerset** · Cottages ornés · *John Nash (1752–1835) · 1804–10 · Various materials, principally rubble stone and brick, stone-tile and thatch roofs · Gift, 1943*

# Stage site

Bury St Edmunds has a long history of theatre, dating from the Middle Ages. In 1608 the Bury Great Fire destroyed the timber Market Cross, hitherto the principal space for performance, along with much of the town centre. By 1725 a permanent theatre had been created on the first floor of the new Market Cross, and in 1774 it was redesigned by Robert Adam as a smart Palladian-style building that survives today. However, soon this was too small and in 1819 William Wilkins opened his Theatre Royal.

The architecturally unpretentious stuccoed Neo-classical building was designed by his architect son William, who also created the National Gallery in London and many Cambridge college buildings. Wilkins's design takes advantage of a naturally sloping site, minimising the need for excavation. The auditorium is encircled by slender, reeded cast-iron columns with acanthus-leaf capitals and Etruscan decoration along the galleries. The existing stage area retains almost all of its original structure: walls, roof, scene dock and proscenium arch, in front of which is the forestage, where performances take place.

Regency theatre was a boisterous, noisy and exciting affair. Audiences talked and heckled throughout. There were trapdoors, waterfalls, drifting clouds, bobbing ships and all manner of sound effects. Scenery would be lowered, and flats slid in from the wings in special grooves. The whole space was lit by oil lamps, which remained in place until the introduction of electricity in 1906. EG

**Theatre Royal, Bury St Edmunds, Suffolk ·**
Neo-classical Regency theatre · *William Wilkins (1778–1839)* · *1819* · *White brick and stucco, slate roof* · *A 999-year lease given by Greene, King & Sons, 1974*

# Cast-iron case

The collecting, cultivation and display of tender plants began to grow in popularity from the late 17th century with the fashion for citrus, planted in large pots and housed in protective 'orangeries' during the colder months. Conservatories differ from these structures as they have beds with permanent indoor planting for the year-round growth of plants that would not survive in the outdoors. Conservatories became increasingly popular with the ready availability of glass through the 19th century.

Sometime before 1810, architect Jeffry Wyatville was brought to Belton to carry out a reworking of the house. Wyatville's design of 1810 for a conservatory (built c.1820) employed the newly discovered structural benefits offered by cast iron, creating a high, airy space within a light frame.

The slender openwork iron columns look improbably delicate. They rise from neat stone plinths and are topped with simple acanthus-leaf capitals, above which sits a hipped iron-framed roof with iron ventilation mechanisms.

The building looks disarmingly modern, its plain ashlar pilasters alternating with tall blocks of glazing, giving it the appearance of a 1930s sunroom. The outer two of the nine bays are narrower, and the balustrade here is solid, subtly accentuating the corners. The large windows are painted dark green, so they appear to recede while the pale ashlar pilasters stand forward.

The two large planting beds house giant palms, camellia and other subtropical plants. At the centre of the building is a pond with a fountain and, to the rear, a boiler house feeds the underfloor hot-air system. EG

**Belton, Lincolnshire** · Neo-classical conservatory · *Jeffry Wyatville (1766–1840)* · *1820* · *Cast-iron frame with ashlar piers, glass roof* · *Gift, 1984*

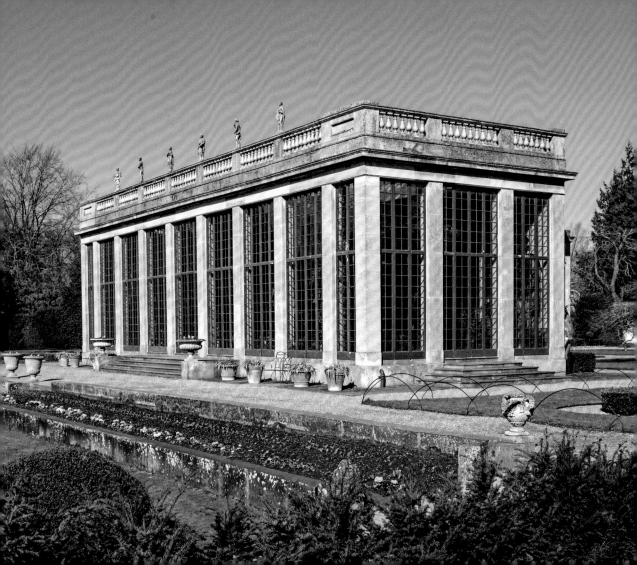

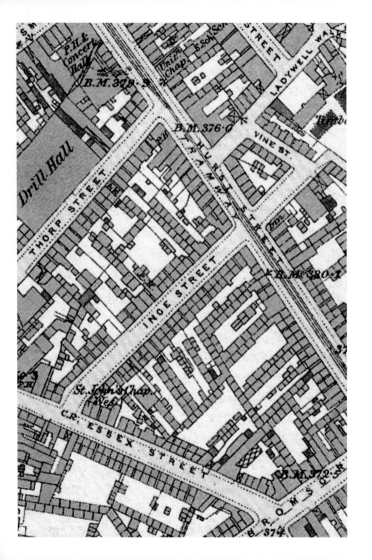

# Hive of industry

Back-to-back housing was developed as a solution to the massive influx of people to cities during the Industrial Revolution. Each home was attached on three sides to a neighbour, with one set of house numbers street-facing and those backing onto them facing into a communal yard. This intensive living inevitably led to poor standards of health and sanitation. The Public Health Act of 1875 permitted municipal corporations to ban new back-to-backs, instead building 'byelaw terraced houses'.

Deep in the commercial heartland of 21st-century Birmingham is Court 15, a little pocket of early industrial urban expansion. A rate levy book of 1823 refers to a lease of 1789 and the first house was built in 1802, divided into two smaller dwellings in the 1820s. Further houses were added to the court, many adapted for commercial use over the following decades.

The back-to-backs are remnants of a housing scheme that dominated the urban landscape from the early 19th century. The block of 11 houses once accommodated up to 60 people around a shared brewhouse for washing and a small row of privies. Each with three floors, the houses typically had a scullery or kitchen on the ground floor, where much of daily life took place, in some cases also acting as a workshop.

Later, the street-facing ground-floor rooms became shops. A narrow winding stair rose to the upper floors and bedrooms.

Standing at the junction between Hurst Street and Inge Street, the court became derelict and dilapidated, although it was still occupied residentially into the 1960s. In 1966 all Birmingham's back-to-backs were condemned. Possibly due to its commercial use, Court 15 is the sole survivor.

The known occupants were typical of Birmingham entrepreneurship, mostly operating their workshops within the home. In 1851 Lawrence Levy, a Jewish watchmaker, moved from London into Court 15 with his family. In the 1860s, Herbert Oldfield, who made glass eyes, lived here. The final occupant was George Saunders, a tailor, who migrated to Birmingham in 1958 from St Kitts and Nevis and ran his shop from number 57 Hurst Street.

Birmingham was at the core of the Industrial Revolution but, in contrast to the northern cities whose success was founded on the mass-production of textiles, Birmingham's productivity was based in small, fine goods. It was a culture of invention, creativity and small workshops – buttons, buckles, silver and enamel. Between 1760 and 1850, Birmingham residents registered over three times as many patents as residents of any other British town or city. The Gun Quarter and Jewellery Quarter are still recognisable districts today. EG

**Court 15, Hurst Street and Inge Street, Birmingham** ·
Back-to-backs · *1820s onwards* · *Red brick, Welsh slate roof* · *Partnership between the National Trust and Birmingham Conservation Trust, 2004*

# Under watchful eyes

Community care for the poor had been formalised under Queen Elizabeth I in 1601 with the allocation of general taxation. The 'impotent poor' (the disabled and elderly) received care in almshouses or poorhouses, while children became apprentices. All those deemed able-bodied were set to work in a house of industry, or workhouse, but those viewed as the 'idle poor' or 'vagrants' were sent to a house of correction, or prison. These conditions largely persisted until the early 19th century.

Originally built as the Thurgarton Hundred Incorporation Workhouse, later known as Southwell Poor Law Union Workhouse and Greet House, this imposing red-brick building was designed by William Nicholson and was a prototype for the many hundreds of workhouses that were built following the passing of the Poor Laws in 1834. The building's cruciform plan was inspired by the planning pattern for prisons that developed in the 18th century at places such as Pentonville and Preston, with four wings projecting from an octagonal hub.

Up to 158 people lived in strictly segregated circumstances, with separate wings of accommodation and exercise yards for men, women and children, all visible from the Master's office in the octagonal central bay.

The general intention was to operate a deterrent system of institutional care, based on strict economy and supervision 'tempered with tenderness towards the Infirm and Guiltless Poor, but opposing by every legal effort the overwhelming Advances of idle, profligate, and sturdy Pauperism' (Rev. Thomas Becher, 1828).

Southwell Workhouse continued in use until 1930, becoming a residential home for the elderly in the 1950s and temporary accommodation for the homeless until 1976. It was purchased by the National Trust in the late 1990s and restored. EG

**The Workhouse, Southwell, Nottinghamshire ·**
*Workhouse · William Nicholson (1803–53) · 1824 ·*
*Red brick, slate roof · Purchased, 1997*

# Gateway to Snowdonia

The 19th century saw the rise of the 'Superstar Engineer', with pioneers such as Isambard Kingdom Brunel (1806–59) and Thomas Telford (1757–1834).

In 1815 Telford was commissioned to improve the mail-coach route from London to Holyhead. In 1817 this was extended to include the Chester leg along the North Wales coast. The English portion simply followed the Roman Watling Street, but the Welsh landscape presented far more challenges, inspiring great engineering works such as the Waterloo Bridge at Betws-y-Coed, embankments through the Ogwen Valley, and the world's first suspension bridges, across the Menai Strait and the Conwy Estuary, both opening in 1826.

The Cob embankment was built from the eastern shore of the Conwy to Yr Ynys, a rocky island in the middle of the river, and the suspension bridge spanned from here to the western shore, where the medieval castle's site provided good foundations.

Conwy Bridge's total span is 99.4 metres and it is 5.4 metres wide. The suspended road deck is carried by eight iron chains, slung from 13-metre-high castellated towers built of Penmon limestone. The road deck was originally paved with pine planks, which were replaced in 1896

with blocks of tropical hardwood. A tarmac surface was introduced in the 1920s to cope with modern traffic. Telford's Bridge remained the only road crossing of the Conwy Estuary, the 'gateway to Snowdonia', until the 1950s and the construction of the Conwy Road Bridge.

The Tollkeeper's House is a miniature castellated Gothick villa, an architectural tribute to the 13th-century Conwy Castle that looms above it. It bears a tablet listing the toll fees to cross the bridge: 'for every horse or beast of draught drawing any Coach, Chariot, Brougham, Clarence, Sociable, Berlin, Calash, Landau, Tandem, Phaeton, Gig, Curricle, Barouche, Whiskey, Buggy or Other Carriage £0 0s 6d'. EG

**Conwy Suspension Bridge, Conwy** · Suspension bridge · *Thomas Telford (1757–1834)* · *1826* · *Wrought iron chains and lattice balustrade, Penmon limestone towers* · *Transferred by Conwy Borough Council, 1965*

*Above* • The suspension bridge with Conwy Castle beyond in an oil painting of 1882, possibly by Edwin Ellis (1842–95) (NT 1319328).

## Vibrant Victorian

The Crown Liquor Saloon – or Crown Bar as it is widely known – is a glittering example of a Victorian gin palace. Dating back to 1826, the street-corner pub has undergone numerous renovations. In 1839 the railway arrived in Belfast and the terminus was built at Great Victoria Street Station, opposite the bar, which took the name of The Ulster Railway Tavern. Its first recorded owner was John O'Hanlon.

The pub was later sold to Michael Flanagan, whose son took charge in 1885, changing the name to The Crown and transforming it into a vibrant gin palace. The brightly tiled façade dates from this period and takes a playful approach to Neo-classical detailing, laced with cherubs, shells, pineapples and stars, while crowns captured in myriad colours and lights declared its new identity.

The Crown is exceptionally richly decorated inside and out, with finely carved woodwork, mosaics and tiling from Craven Dunnill of Bridgnorth in Shropshire. Stained, etched and mirrored glass was provided by the many specialist manufacturers and suppliers in Belfast at the time, including those who would have been employed in fitting out the ships being built in the Belfast docks. By day, sunlight animates the stained glass; by night, gaslights

bring a glow to the red granite and highly polished wood surfaces. Cast-iron columns mimic the trunks of palm trees with Corinthian acanthus-leaf capitals. Birds are painted on mirror glass panels and heraldic wooden beasts prowl the tops of the partitions around the ten miniature snugs. These drinking booths, for discreet conversations, undisturbed drinking or secretive liaisons, are lettered A–J and furnished with a bell system for alerting staff that their occupants are in need of sustenance.

Poet and architectural campaigner Sir John Betjeman (1906–84) brought attention to The Crown, describing it as 'a many-coloured cavern' in his BBC documentary *Betjeman's Belfast* in 1976. EG

**The Crown, Belfast, County Antrim** · Gin palace · *E. & J. Byrne, Belfast · 1826 · Brick with majolica tiling and mosaic, slate roof · Acquired with local funds and with the co-operation of Bass Ireland, 1978*

# D-Day in Dunwich

The Preventive Water Guard was established in 1809 at the height of the Napoleonic Wars, initially to counteract smuggling. It became the Coastguard in 1822 and later, in 1856, passed under the control of the Admiralty, which reused the south coast's defensive Martello Towers as housing for the coastguards. Where no towers existed, as at Dunwich Heath, new barracks were built.

Appearing on the tithe map of 1839, the cottages date from *c*.1835, possibly replacing earlier timber structures. Seven cottages were built using Flemish-bond brickwork, with walls tarred like ships' hulls for protection against the elements.

During the Second World War, the cottages were extended and adapted to incorporate a battery observation post and radar station. In 1943 the site became host to Operation Kruschen, testing ways of breaching German defences in preparation for the D-Day landings. The operation saw a complete mock German defensive position constructed, including trenches, minefields, pillboxes, weapon-pits and anti-tank measures. EG

**Dunwich Heath, Suffolk** · Coastguard's cottages · *c.1835 · Tarred (now painted) brick and concrete, slate roofs · Neptune Purchase, 1968*

# Norman conquest

The Welsh word *penrhyn* literally means promontory, and this massive Neo-Norman castle stands on just such a piece of land, reaching out into the Menai Strait. The land was given to Goronwy ap Ednyfed (d.1268) and in the early 15th-century aftermath of the Glyndŵr uprising, his descendants, the Gruffudds, built a fine hall house on the land. We know from praise poetry that it had a tower, was brightly limewashed and that it included a chapel – part of which survives. The bones of that medieval house are still embedded in the core of Penrhyn Castle today.

Richard Pennant (1739–1808) was to establish the Penrhyn name as a pioneering industrialist and developer of the world's largest slate quarry, Penrhyn Quarry at nearby Bethesda. Pennant was descended from Gifford Pennant, who had owned sugarcane plantations in Jamaica in the 17th century. He married Anna Susannah Warburton of the Gruffudd line but they died childless and in 1816 George Hay Dawkins inherited the estate and took the name Pennant. He brought with him the Jamaican sugar fortune, which was supplemented in 1835 by a payment of £14,683 through a government scheme that compensated the former owners of enslaved people, while offering no compensation whatsoever to those who had been enslaved.

*Above* · This lithograph by George Hawkins the Younger (1819–1852) shows two hunting dogs at the foot of the Grand Staircase at Penrhyn Castle in 1846, just a few years after construction was completed (NT 1420632.7).

In around 1820, Dawkins-Pennant commissioned the architect Thomas Hopper to design a new house, perhaps inspired by Edward I's castles at Caernarfon, Beaumaris and Conwy. The choice of the Romanesque style was unusual, with the only real precedent being Hopper's smaller version at Gosford in County Armagh. Externally austere, the keep owes much to the Norman Tower of London or Hedingham Castle in Essex, but inside, apart from its huge scale and lack of apparent intimacy, Penrhyn does have a softer side. Here we see Hopper embrace local skills and materials. Chimneypieces are carved from multicoloured Môn marble, and Hopper showcased Penrhyn slate in intricately carved side tables and at least two beds.

The castle walls have brick at their core, clad in Penmon limestone, with a vast roof slated from Penrhyn Quarry. Each of the massively proportioned spaces is decorated with chevrons, fantastical beast heads, huge cluster columns and cushion capitals. Hopper surely perfected his command of Neo-Norman detailing at Penrhyn, as it was lavished not only on the building itself but on furniture, lighting and carpets alike. EG

**Penrhyn Castle, Gwynedd** · Neo-Norman castle · *Thomas Hopper (1776–1856)* · *1820s–40s* · *Brick carcass with Penmon limestone ashlar, slate and lead roof* · *National Land Fund, 1951*

# Small but perfectly formed

The old castle at Crom was built in the early 17th century for Michael Balfour, who arrived from Scotland under the Ulster Plantations. The castle survived two sieges by the Jacobites in 1689 but burned down in 1764 and the family moved away from the site. In the 19th century additional walls and towers were added to the ruins of the old castle for romantic effect.

In 1831 John Crichton, 3rd Earl of Erne, commissioned architect Edward Blore (1787–1879), who would later work on Buckingham Palace, to build a new 'Tudor-Gothic' castle. It was completed in 1838. However, in 1841 this too burned down and Dublin architect George Sudden was drafted in to rescue Crom.

Sudden rebuilt the house largely to Blore's design and then turned his hand to creating a boathouse, also in the Tudor-Gothic style to complement the castle. The Boathouse is raised above the lakeside, with a slipway to the front giving access onto the water. The ground-floor stonework is rusticated with a pair of stone buttresses flanking the boatshed doorway. A crenelated parapet above surrounds the viewing platform upon which sits the pretty, if bijou, house.

Ornate bargeboards frame the lakeside gable and geometric castings are used for the projecting window here and to other elevations. A cluster of three moulded chimneys and slender finials to the ridge add interest to the roofline. The picturesque character of the building harmonises well with the surrounding landscape, which was the work of the English landscaper W.S. Gilpin. EG

**Crom Boathouse, County Fermanagh** · Tudor-Gothic-style boathouse · *George Sudden (active c.1830–50)* · *1840s* · *Rusticated sandstone, slate roof* · *Gift, 1987*

# From muzzle-loaders to missiles

The Needles, overlooking both the Solent and the English Channel, commands a strategically advantageous position. The Old Battery was built between 1861 and 1863 as one of Lord Palmerston's 'Follies', a series of fortifications built along the English south coast in response to increasingly hostile activity by France.

The Old Battery is largely built of brick and concrete, with six semi-circular gun emplacements, originally equipped with 7-inch (178mm) Armstrong rifled breech-loading guns. In 1873 these were replaced with 9-inch (229mm) rifled muzzle-loading guns and the old guns thrown into the sea, to be rescued by the National Trust in 1982 and put on display. By the 1890s, the New Battery had been built further up the cliff because it was feared that the more powerful modern guns might cause the soft chalk to collapse.

In 1899 a searchlight emplacement was built, and a battery command post was added between 1900 and 1902, continuing to serve this role until after the Second World War. Britain's first anti-aircraft gun was tested on the parade ground in 1913.

With the advent of the Cold War and the nuclear threat from the Soviet Union, the High Down site was developed for rocket testing. A new concrete test area was built with the New Battery being used for offices. Black Knight rockets tested here contributed towards the successful launch of Britain's Prospero satellite in 1971. EG

**The Needles Old Battery and New Battery, High Down Test Site, Isle of Wight** · Coastal defence battery and rocket test site · *1860s, 1890s, 1956–7 · Concrete, brick, steel · Anonymous donor and Neptune funds, 1975, and the Commander Parker Memorial Fund, 1976*

# Whatever looks best *is* best

William Burges was the most exuberantly imaginative of Gothic Revival architects, convinced that 'Whatever looks best *is* best'. Knightshayes Court was his only entirely new country house. Sir John Heathcoat Amory (1829–1914) commissioned it in 1869 for his newly purchased estate overlooking Tiverton and the family's lace net factory.

Burges used local red Hensley stone with golden Ham Hill stone dressings and red clay tiles. His skilfully asymmetrical composition has a massive staircase tower – lower and less dominant than initially planned – steep roofs, gables and chimneys, creating a varied skyline. The elevations express the interior plan – a key Gothic Revival principle: the Great Hall has Gothic-traceried arched windows, a tall bay window and separate roof.

High Victorian 'muscular' details, inspired by the 13th-century French buildings Burges loved, include plate tracery that looks as though it has been punched through solid stone. The playful touches are typical Burges: the Billiard Room has a frieze of stone balls. Burges's fine sculpture, carved by his favoured sculptor Thomas Nicholls (*c.*1825–96), features strongly. Gargoyles and fantastic beasts enliven the façades. The Hall's open timber roof has

stone corbels 'representing the conditions of Life', from peasants to a king and queen. In the Billiard Room, animal corbels symbolise the Seven Deadly Sins.

Burges's vision for the interior was never fully realised. In 1873 Heathcoat Amory rejected his inventive designs (still at Knightshayes) for colourful rooms rich with sculpture, stained glass and mural painting. Instead, prestigious decorator J.D. Crace (1838–1919) incorporated some of Burges's details into more conventional, less extravagant Gothic interiors, completed in 1883. Just a few years later, the Drawing Room's elaborate ceiling was covered up. Burges's Hall screen was subsequently removed. After 1945, Sir John and Lady Heathcoat Amory removed and covered up many Gothic features. Since 1973, the National Trust has restored the splendour of the principal rooms, adding a huge Burges fireplace relocated from Worcester College, Oxford. SP

**Knightshayes Court, Devon** · Gothic Revival mansion ·
*William Burges (1827–81)* · *1869–83* · *Red Hensley stone, golden Ham Hill stone dressings, red clay-tile roofs* · *Bequest, 1972*

# For those in peril

For at least 2,000 years, the safety of mariners navigating treacherous coasts was reliant on well-stoked fires held in stone towers. The Pharos of Alexandria, fragments of which survive beneath the Mediterranean waves, was built during the reign of Ptolemy Philadelphus II (309–246BC) and is depicted in mosaics and on coins as a towering square-based, stepped structure, holding aloft a flame. The architecture of historic lighthouses is well-recorded and documented in literature, but rarely is this ancient source of their saviour flame acknowledged.

Trinity House, the organisation that oversees lighthouses, was established in 1514, initially to regulate and improve the standards of piloting on the River Thames. In 1609 Trinity House built its first lighthouse, a pair of wooden towers with candle illumination, at Lowestoft, on the notorious Newcastle-to-London coal route.

Leap forward another 260 years to 1871, and the UK's first lighthouse designed to use alternating electric current, the most advanced lighthouse of its day, was built at Souter between the Tyne and Wear estuaries. Souter stands guard over the ships pouring forth, loaded with precious cargo, from the Tyne Estuary. The complex was designed by Trinity House's Resident Engineer James N. Douglass, and

includes an engine house with powerful foghorn. The majestic lighthouse, a 22-metre tapered tower painted in red and white stripes, faces east, to keep ships off the rocks below Marsden Cliffs and the reefs of the Whitburn Steel. A bright, white rendered quadrangle, roofed in Welsh slate, sits at its feet, accommodating engines, boilers, workshops and housing.

Internally, a giddying series of spiral staircases and ladders give access to the lantern room at the top of the building.

Souter's original bifocal lens is still in situ. When it was first lit, Souter was described as 'without doubt one of the most powerful lights in the world'. EG

**Souter Lighthouse, Tyne and Wear** · Electric lighthouse · *1871 · Rendered masonry, slate roofs · Acquired with a donation from the Baring Foundation, a bequest from Mrs G.I. Windmill and Enterprise Neptune Funds, 1990*

# Chateau Rothschild

With its intricately worked golden stone glowing in the sunshine, Waddesdon Manor masquerades as a Loire Valley chateau with effortless ease. However, the story of this exceptional building begins with a family emerging from the Jewish ghetto in Frankfurt.

It was here that Mayer Amschel Rothschild (1744–1812) established an enterprise dealing in antiquities that was to become one of the most successful financial businesses in the world. Joined by his five sons, the ensuing years saw Rothschild banks established in five European cities, and the dynasty was born. The family wealth grew to such an extent that the bank was able to fund the Duke of Wellington's Waterloo campaign in 1815.

The Waddesdon estate was bought in 1874 by Baron Ferdinand de Rothschild (1839–98), of the Vienna branch of the family, from the Duke of Marlborough. It was an unremarkable agricultural estate, but between 1874 and 1889 it was transformed by the addition of an extraordinary house and garden, built as a weekend retreat, a place to entertain guests and to house Rothschild's burgeoning art collections.

Rothschild wanted the exterior of his house to reflect the style of the chateaux of the Loire Valley, so he engaged French architect Gabriel-

Hippolyte Destailleur to execute this feat. Destailleur borrowed detail with enthusiasm: the spiral staircase turrets from Chambord and Blois; the pinnacled dormers from Azay-le-Rideau and Chenonceau; round and square turrets, steep roofs and upswept eaves from Maintenon. Waddesdon Manor – a French Renaissance chateau in Buckinghamshire – was complete.

Historicising style continued inside, but in contrast, inspired by the 18th century. Here, decorative elements include panelling taken from Parisian townhouses. The rooms are relentlessly sumptuous, with richly gilded woodwork and cornices and finely moulded plasterwork, an appropriate setting for Rothschild's magnificent collections of decorative and fine art.

While taking an antiquarian approach to visible design, Destailleur employed the latest architectural technologies behind the scenes. The building has a steel frame, enabling different floorplans at ground- and first-floor levels. The house had gas-fired central heating and lighting, hot and cold running water and it was electrified in the 1890s. EG

**Waddesdon Manor, Buckinghamshire** · French chateau · *Gabriel-Hippolyte Destailleur (1822–93)* · *1874–89* · *Bath stone and brick, slate and lead roof* · *Bequest, 1957*

# Cathedral in miniature

'A cathedral in miniature' is an apt description for Clumber Chapel. This exceptional example of the Gothic Revival was designed by G.F. Bodley for the 7th Duke of Newcastle (1864–1928) between 1886 and 1889.

The style is 'Decorated', the 14th-century medieval style in revival, and perfectly executed in the soaring 55-metre spire, vaulting, columns and arcades, and magnificent east window tracery. The plan is cruciform, both nave and chancel of four bays, flanked at the east end by a Lady chapel, sacristy and vestry.

The 7th Duke was a follower of the Anglo-Catholic movement and building this chapel was an act of devotion. It is filled with iconography in carving and sculpture, as well as in the choice of scenes represented in the windows. The stained glass was designed by C.E. Kempe (1837–1907), a pupil and frequent collaborator with Bodley.

The chapel, stable block, Duke's Study and Bow Corridor are the only built reminder that this was once the magnificent home of the Dukes of Newcastle. The voluptuous 18th-century Italianate palace was badly damaged by fire in 1879, and finally demolished in 1938. EG

**Clumber, Nottinghamshire** · Gothic Revival chapel · *G.F. Bodley (1827–1907) · 1886-9 · Polychromatic Steetley and Runcorn sandstone ashlar, lead roofs · Purchase, 1946*

## Vernacular Arts and Crafts

Ernest Gimson was an architect whose design philosophy was embedded in the principles of the Arts and Crafts movement. In 1898 his brother Sydney asked Ernest to design a holiday home in the Charnwood Forest area outside Leicester, the date recorded 'G 1899' in the slate lintel above the front door.

Stoneywell appears to emerge organically from its stony hillside, wrapped around by a billowing blanket of bilberry bushes, now very much a feature of the garden, although only introduced by Sydney's grandson. The house has a meandering, soft form, which follows the contours of the site, with windows apparently inserted arbitrarily. However, this is a carefully considered composition, albeit one altered from its original appearance by the addition of a Swithland slate roof, following a terrible thatch fire in 1939. This was carried out sensitively, though, retaining even the slate verge to the gable wall as it appears in the watercolour that hangs on the kitchen wall. The little eyebrow windows typical of a thatched roof were replaced with the larger dormers we see today, allowing more sunlight to flood into the rooms.

Internally, Stoneywell also moves with the landscape, with almost every room on a different level, each unfolding beyond a curiously shaped

step or curving corridor. The architectural
historian Nicholas Cooper writes that,

*There is the most extraordinary visual, structural
and functional logic to Stoneywell. Of course, there
is the other structural and functional logic that says:
Build a house of brick on level ground – but that is
the difference between building and architecture.*

Many of the pieces of furniture were designed
and made by Gimson, entirely in the spirit of the
Arts and Crafts movement, whose adherents
believed in the honesty and beauty of the hand-
made and the inferiority of mass-production.

The Stoneywell brand of Arts and Crafts
borrows cleverly from vernacular architecture,
using local materials to establish an ancient
and natural relationship with the surrounding
landscape. Externally, the massive, stepped
stone chimney stack suggests medieval origins.
Internally, however, the inscription 'SAG JLG
1899' over the fireplace and reading niche
reveals the truth. EG

**Stoneywell, Leicestershire** · Arts and Crafts house
· *Ernest Gimson (1864–1919)* · *1899* · *Stone, slate roof,
originally thatched* · *Purchased, 2012*

# A monument to beer

These enormous 19th-century hop-drying buildings demonstrate the industrialisation of a rural enterprise, and the magnitude of the hop's economic importance. It was the demand for hop flowers, which give beer its distinctive flavour and aroma, that brought this vigorous native climbing plant into cultivation all over Europe for the last millennium and introduced this form of building into the English countryside.

Bought in 1930, the then amateur gardeners Vita Sackville-West (1892–1962) and Harold Nicolson (1886–1968) created here at Sissinghurst one of the world's most sensational gardens, incorporating the ruinous remains of 500 years of other occupiers' lives: a Tudor house, an Elizabethan manor, and more utilitarian farm buildings. They are not silent witnesses, and visitors find evidence of surprising histories: Sissinghurst as prisoner of war camp, workhouse, home for farm labourers and farmstead. Beyond the high, clipped hedges and romantic 'garden rooms', visitors encounter another unexpected monument, to one of Britain's great pleasures – beer.

For Sissinghurst in another life grew hops for brewing. To prevent the freshly picked hop flowers heating naturally, which would drive off the essential oils and therefore their flavour and value, hops need to be dried quickly with hot air and brisk ventilation. They were brought to buildings like these (called 'oasts' in Kent and Sussex, but 'hop kilns' in Herefordshire and Worcestershire) to achieve this. Under the six pyramidal roofs, topped with wooden cowls turned by the wind to encourage air flow, green hops were thinly raked in batches over perforated upper floors, to permit hot air to rise from fires below (the two drying kilns with a circular plan, locally known as 'roundels', are slightly earlier in date but operated in the same way). The heated hops were then spread to cool in the interconnected rectangular building, the 'stowage', before being tightly compressed into jute bags or 'pockets' for transport to a brewery. JG

**Oast Houses, Sissinghurst, Kent** · Hop-drying kilns · *Late 19th century · Red brick, clay-tile roofs · Transferred through the National Land Fund, 1967*

# Ancient and modern

At Castle Drogo, perched dramatically above the Teign Gorge, architect Edwin Lutyens created a masterpiece. According to the architectural historian Christopher Hussey, 'The ultimate justification of Drogo is that it does not pretend to be a castle. It is a castle, as a castle is built, of granite, on a mountain, in the twentieth century.'

The client was Julius Drewe (1856–1931), founder of the Home and Colonial Stores, whose desire was to connect with his supposed ancient Devonian roots by establishing an 'ancestral seat' in the manner of a medieval castle. However, this castle was to come complete with modern comforts, sleek lines and an architectural style fully identifiable as that of Edwin Lutyens, prominent architect of the moment.

Begun in 1911, initial plans were for a large castle arranged around the north, east and west sides of a 'splayed' courtyard, not unlike Goddards, Lutyens's Surrey house of 1898–1900. However, changes to the design, for example Drewe's request to thicken the walls, added to the cost and the west range was abandoned early on. Progress fell victim to a sparsity of workmen following the outbreak of the First World War, which would go on to claim the life of Drewe's son Adrian on 12 July 1917. After this, much of Drewe's passion for the project was lost.

The resulting version of Drogo is about a third of its intended extent. The north range Great Hall was abandoned, and its footings became an undercroft chapel. Drogo was finally completed in 1930. During the elapsed two decades, Lutyens had created many Imperial buildings in India, reworked Lindisfarne Castle (completed 1914) and, poignantly, designed many war memorials, including the huge and sombre Thiepval Arch (1928–32), all of which have echoes of Castle Drogo.

Despite its circuitous journey to completion, Castle Drogo is a remarkable piece of architecture. Thoughtful detailing runs throughout the house, with Drewe lions appearing in door catches, rainwater hoppers and, more formally, in a low-relief carved tablet above the front door. This edifice is calculated to lend age and authenticity to the Drewe name and estate, while doing so in a suave, modern manner. EG

**Castle Drogo, Devon** · Medieval Revival castle · *Edwin Lutyens (1869–1944) · 1911–30 · Granite walls and roof · Drewe Gift, 1974*

# Wind-powered wonder

Horsey Windpump is the youngest of the drainage mills that have been so vital to maintaining the unique landscape of the Norfolk Broads since the 18th century. Alongside their primary function as drainage pumps, many of the wind-driven mills were also used as part of a secret warning system designed to alert the wherry boats moving smuggled goods from the coast to Norwich. If the sails were positioned in an 'x' the wherryman knew to hide the contraband as the excise men had been spotted.

Various mills have stood on this site since around the middle of the 18th century. The present four-storey redbrick windpump, rebuilt in 1912 by millwright Edwin William Daniel England of Ludham (known as Dan England), contains many elements of the previous 1826 mill. Horsey mill was vital to the drainage effort when the North Sea repeatedly breached the sand dunes in 1938. In 1943 the mill was struck by lightning. The windpump was replaced by its diesel back-up pump and, subsequently,

by the electric one used today. The mill was purchased by the National Trust in 1948 and eventually restored between 1961 and 1964 after a fundraising campaign organised by the Society for the Protection of Ancient Buildings. The mill was damaged in the Great Storm of 1987 and has undergone various repair and restoration projects, most recently in 2016–19.

Today, Horsey Windpump stands as a monument to the lives and livelihoods once sustained by this unique landscape, a survivor of the historic Broads panorama of marshland punctuated by medieval churches and mills. SH

**Horsey Windpump, Norfolk** · Wind-powered drainage mill · *Dan England (c.1850–1933)* · *1912* · *Brick, timber weatherboarding* · *Purchased, 1948*

# Portmeirion's Irish cousin

In 1912, Cushendun, a scattered hamlet of houses facing a small harbour on the Antrim coast, was transformed by Welsh architect Clough Williams-Ellis in a late flourishing of Arts and Crafts style.

Williams-Ellis was commissioned by Ronald McNeill, Lord Cushendun (1861–1934), to build a series of tenantry houses, beginning with The Square. In the early 1920s, after the IRA set fire to Glenmona Lodge, McNeill's seaside villa at Cushendun, it was Williams-Ellis who was asked to redesign the house. In 1925 he completed Maud Cottages for McNeill, in memory of Maud Bolitho, Lady Cushendun (1859–1925).

Best known for Portmeirion – his 'Italianate' village in North Wales – Williams-Ellis was liberal and creative in his employment of architectural vocabulary. At Cushendun he chose an approachable form of Arts and Crafts. Pairs of small-paned casements, some with shutters, and split stable doors add to the impression of 'cottaginess'. The use of hanging slates is not a local tradition but was commonplace in Williams-Ellis's homeland of North Wales. Some of his early architectural drawings prefigure many of the details at Cushendun. Early images of Cushendun show shutters and doors painted in shades of green and blue, a similar colour palette to that used at Portmeirion and Williams-Ellis's Brondanw Estate.

The arcaded doorways and shallow curvature of the projecting bay of Maud Cottages and the apex roundel on the axial gable of The Square unite them and stamp Williams-Ellis's signature on these buildings. EG

**The Square and Maud Cottages, Cushendun, County Antrim** · Arts and Crafts terraces · *Clough Williams-Ellis (1883–1978) · 1912 and 1925 · Rendered masonry, slate hanging and slate roofs · Acquired through Ulster Land Fund, 1953*

# Suburban star

Between the First and Second World Wars, the shape of towns and cities changed dramatically. The dreams and ambitions of the nation had been transformed by the experience of the First World War, and the Great Depression had brought about a determined shift towards investing in the certainty of bricks and mortar. Mortgages became accessible even to those on relatively low incomes, placing home-ownership within reach of the majority of the population.

Between 1919 and 1930 approximately four million new homes were built in England, both to meet the need for council housing and by developers selling to first-time homeowners. The suburb was born. Inspiration was taken from the garden-city movement – housing built on the fringes of a city, a hybrid of countryside and urban living. Short rows or pairs of houses, with front gardens and bay windows, were built around closes, along avenues and short drives. Space, light and fresh air were available and to be enjoyed.

In 1919 Liverpool contained some of the worst slum housing in the country. During the interwar period between 1918 and 1939, Liverpool became the first city to invest in council housing, building 33,000 new homes to accommodate 140,000 local residents.

*Above* · John Lennon as a child standing outside Mendips, 251 Menlove Avenue, in the early 1950s.

Mendips, 251 Menlove Avenue, in the Woolton suburb of Liverpool, was built in 1933 by J.W. Jones and Sons Ltd, a firm of building contractors responsible for many of the houses in the local area, all similarly styled with typical rendered walls, hipped roofs and generous bay windows. Decorative features such as the stained-glass details in windows and front door, tiled fire surrounds and black-and-white indoor bathroom all survive.

From 1946 to 1963 Mendips was the home of John Lennon (1940–80), where he lived with his aunt and uncle, Mimi and George Smith. EG

**Mendips, Liverpool** · Suburban semi-detached house · *J.W. Jones and Sons Ltd · 1933 · Rendered brick, clay-tile roof · Yoko Ono Gift, 2002*

# High-tech hideaway

Designed as a caravan without wheels, The Shack provided a peaceful sanctuary for its designers, the architectural duo Seely & Paget. After meeting as students at the University of Cambridge, John Seely, 2nd Baron Mottistone (1899–1963), and Paul Paget (1901–85) lived and worked together until Seely's death, habitually referring to each other as 'the partner'. The Shack was built on the Isle of Wight and was kept on Seely's family estate, overlooking the sea near Freshwater, before moving to the grounds of Mottistone Manor when he inherited it.

From the outside, The Shack looks rather basic – resting on staddle stones with wooden planks for walls and a cedar-shingle roof. Internally, however, 'is where the fun starts' according to Paget. It is equipped as a 1930s gadget-lover's paradise, with contemporary labour-saving devices built in, including a self-winding clock above the gas fire and even a shower. The fittings (below left) are of high-quality; chrome ladders provide access to the single bunks at either end of the room with their electric reading lamps, while each partner also had their own desk to work at.

The two architects described it as a place where they could get away from the hustle and bustle of modern life and the office, while still having all the modern conveniences they were used to. It also provided a place for them to continue living their joint professional and personal lives together, while taking a break from the city. GR

**The Shack, Mottistone Manor, Isle of Wight ·**
Architects' office · *Seely & Paget · c.1934 · Timber frame raised on staddle stones, walls and roof clad with Canadian cedar shingles · Paul Paget Gift, 1985*

# Tailor-made

The architectural historian Neil Bingham has likened The Homewood to an exquisitely tailored Savile Row suit. There is something so stylish about its form, sleek about its setting and glamorous about its interiors.

Patrick Gwynne's parents moved to Esher, Surrey, a year after his birth, renting then buying a Victorian house in grounds that would later be used to site The Homewood. Gwynne had become excited about Modernism while still at school and later worked with Wells Coates (1895–1958), one of the founders of the Modern Architectural Research Group and architect of the Isokon Flats (1933–4) in Hampstead.

Gwynne began designing the home for his parents in 1937, at just 24 years of age, and would go on to live in it himself until his death in 2003. Clearly inspired by Le Corbusier's Villa Savoie, the first floor is elevated on piloti, creating a canopied entrance and carport beneath.

The design makes use throughout of materials much associated with the Modernist movement – concrete piers, vertical plate glass and glass bricks, all below flat concrete roofs. Bedrooms are on the upper floor to the left, the service wing to the right and, at the centre, just off the hall, a sophisticated spiral staircase with its

terrazzo finish, which curves around a circular floor uplighter.

The interiors were tailored to the needs of the architect's parents, sister and, later, himself. The materials are as carefully considered as those of the construction (if a little more luxurious): doors padded with white leather, built-in wall units veneered in walnut (later replaced with Indian laurel), tambour doors, walls of black Levanto marble, and a painted screen used to divide the living and dining rooms when needed, all of them carefully lit. They form the perfect backdrop to the furniture collection (some of it designed by Gwynne himself) and create an ideal setting for entertaining. LP

**The Homewood, Surrey** · Modernist house · *Patrick Gwynne (1913–2003)* · *1938–9* · *Concrete, glass and brick* · *Gift, 1999*

# Cold War warrior

The Cold War decades of the mid-20th century saw a proliferation of structures housing secret activities. As the threat of nuclear war began to escalate, so did the need to develop and test atomic weapons. The site chosen was Europe's largest vegetated shingle spit, off the Suffolk coast. Parts of it are regularly inundated, and the whole landscape is constantly on the move.

The atomic testing laboratories at Orford Ness inhabit their shifting landscape with a quiet air of dignified decay. Mass concrete roofs and bunker-like walls, buttressed by shingle banks, rusting steel girders and peeling paint serve as ghostly reminders of the fragility of international peace.

During the mid-1930s, a team led by Robert Watson-Watt used Orford Ness's remoteness to create the Ionospheric Research Station – cover for the development of the aerial defence system that became known as radar. Later, between 1954 and 1956, the Atomic Weapons Research Establishment constructed three laboratories and the Control Room to Laboratory 1. Laboratory 1 has a 30-metre-long chamber at its heart, with a lightweight steel-framed roof atop massively constructed concrete walls buried in shingle, intended to force accidental blast vertically rather than laterally. The yawning entrance is reminiscent of the tomb of Agamemnon or the

lair of a Bond villain. This is where development and testing took place of Britain's initial nuclear capability, known as Blue Danube.

Phase 2 of testing, from 1960, brought the Vibration Test Buildings, now known as 'the pagodas', and their Centrifuge. This is where the first generation of Polaris missiles was born. In 1962 the final phase of building included the Munitions Storage Magazine, with its barrel-vaulted concrete roof, and the Hard Impact Facility, in which a weapon, minus its fissile core, was propelled by a rocket-powered sled against a concrete wall.

There is but a narrow margin between their celebrated architectural cousins, Modernist mansions, and these fading remnants of the Cold War, left to return to the earth and be reclaimed by nature.

Robert Macfarlane's poem 'Ness' vividly evokes the unique atmosphere of this place: 'Shingle shelters bunker, bunker shelters blast / Dark drifts down, night flies fast'. EG

**Orford Ness Atomic Research Facility, Suffolk** · Military testing structures · *Atomic Weapons Research Establishment (Phase 1: C.W. Glover and Partners, Phase 2: G.W. Dixon)* · *1954–69* · *Reinforced concrete* · *Purchased, 1993*

# When building becomes landscape

One of the youngest structures in the ownership of the National Trust, the Giant's Causeway Visitor Centre, completed in 2012, is both bold and highly sensitive to its surroundings. The vertiginous black basalt external walls echo the basalt columns of the Causeway and, inside, mass concrete slabs allow cool slices of light to slip across the floor and ceiling. Every surface is polished and reflective, smooth like the rock and water of the surrounding environment.

Creating a large building in a wide-open landscape presents an exciting challenge to the architect. Heneghan Peng's building achieves the necessary balance between showing an open, welcoming face and laying only a gentle hand on its setting. The huge structure is semi-underground, its flat grassy roofs blending into the landscape and then tilting up sharply, mimicking the columns of the Causeway itself. Or, in the words of the architects, 'There is no longer a building and landscape, but building becomes landscape and the landscape itself remains spectacular and iconic'. EG

**Giant's Causeway Visitor Centre, County Antrim ·**
Visitor centre · *Heneghan Peng Architects · 2012 · Basalt, concrete, glass, grass roof · National Trust built, with external funding support*

# Glossary of terms

**Alabaster** · Fine-grained white stone used for carving. The Green Velvet Room at Hardwick has panelling of alabaster and blackstone. Stunning alabaster-work can also be seen in the Marble Hall at Kedleston, which is based on a Roman atrium, with soaring, fluted alabaster columns.

**Arcade** · Series of arches supported on columns or piers, often supporting a roof over a covered walkway. When used close against a wall, for decorative purposes, it is known as a blind arcade. Powis Castle's Aviary is in the form of an arcade, while Maud Terrace at Cushendun has blind arcading to its central projecting bay.

**Arcadian** · Idealised natural landscape, often populated by shepherds, nymphs and other mythical beings. Arcadia is an area in central Greece, which was said to be the innocent and unspoiled home of Hermes and Pan. This led to its use in popular culture to define a place of harmonious, natural beauty, thus translated into the English Landscape Garden, as exemplified at Stourhead and Croome.

**Arts and Crafts** · Born out of a dissatisfaction with increasing mechanisation and the mass-production of decorative art objects, the movement was centred around designer-philosopher William Morris, artists Edward Burne-Jones and Ford Madox Brown, and architect Philip Webb. They believed in truth to material, beauty in functionality and the integrity of a maker who was committed to seeing the process through from inception to completion. They strove to integrate the fine and decorative arts and put them on an equal footing. The Red House, Standen and Stoneywell exemplify the Arts and Crafts movement.

**Ashlar** · Stone-block finish, with straight-cut edges and slim mortar joints.

**Balustrade** · A row of uprights (or balusters) supporting a handrail or as part of a parapet, etc.

**Bay** · Section or subdivision of a building, such as the repeated parts of a façade between pilasters, etc., or of a roof between trusses; the architectural subdivisions of a church between buttresses, piers, etc.

**Boss** · Decorative feature at the intersection of structural ribwork in a stone vault, such as Lacock's cloister, or in a decorative plaster ceiling, such as Chastleton's Great Chamber or Wray Castle's Music Room. Bosses are often decorated with foliage, coats of arms or figures, as in the late medieval oak bosses at Rufford Old Hall.

**Brace** · Diagonal or curved timber component that lends lateral strength to a roof structure, where it is referred to as a windbrace, or in a timber-framed building, such as Alfriston Clergy

House. At Lytes Cary, Speke and Rufford Old Hall, the roof has multiple layers of windbraces.

**Broken pediment** · In Classical architecture, a decorative framing feature over an opening from which the apex is missing. It can be arched, as seen at Belton's chapel, rendered in wood painted to imitate marble, or triangular in form, as seen over the windows at Lodge Park and the stable entrance at Tredegar.

**Capital** · Gothic or Classical decorative feature at the top of a column or pilaster. Norman examples at Horton Court, either side of the doorway, take the form of a simple cushion, slightly scalloped. In the Classical or Neo-classical context, capitals are defined by different styles: Doric, Ionic, Corinthian, Tuscan or Composite. *See* **Classical orders**

**Chancel** · The space around the altar at the east end of the church, sometimes separated from the main body of a church, the nave, by a screen, steps, or a change in roof level. Also, sometimes a more highly decorated part of the building. The chancel at Fountains Abbey houses nine altars and is in the form of a pair of transepts. More typical examples can be seen at St Mary the Virgin, Clumber, and the Chapel of the Holy Trinity, Staunton Harold.

**Chevron** · Serrated, zig-zag pattern of decoration often seen in Norman mouldings. At Horton Court,

*Left* · The **braced** roof of Rufford Old Hall, a remarkable Tudor house in Lancashire.

the round head of the 12th-century doorway on the south elevation is detailed using a chevron pattern. Thomas Hopper used the same pattern 700 years later at Neo-Norman Penrhyn Castle.

**Chimneypiece** · Often ornate surround to a fireplace. The Drawing Room at Cragside features a particularly dramatic example in marble of c.1882 by R. Norman Shaw. Sometimes incorporates a framed element above – the overmantel.

**Choir** · The area of grander ecclesiastical buildings where singing takes place, sometimes one and the same as the chancel. Fountains Abbey and Clumber both have choirs, built some 700 years apart.

**Classical orders** · Doric is the earliest and simplest of the Greek orders, followed by Ionic, which is characterised by ram's horns or 'volutes', and Corinthian, in which the capitals are decorated with acanthus leaves. In addition to the three principal Greek orders, Tuscan is a simple Roman order and Composite is a combination of Ionic and Corinthian. The orders define a set arrangement of decorative details from top to bottom of a column, as found in ancient Greek and Roman architecture and copied by the architects who developed the Neo-classical style, from the late Baroque of Sir John Vanbrugh (Seaton Delaval), through the Palladianism of Robert Adam (Croome, Saltram, Kedleston) and James Paine (Nostell, Gibside Chapel).

**Coffered** · Decorated with a recessed rectangular or polygonal design, for example on the underside of a ceiling or dome, as in Mussenden Temple or the staircase at The Vyne.

**Corbel** · Projecting block of stone or piece of timber that supports a beam or other structural element. Fine Gothic Revival examples can be found at Knightshayes Court. A row of similar supports running the length of a wall is called a corbel course. A corbel course with gaps through which to drop missiles is a defensive feature called a machicolation, as seen at Tattershall Castle. Whole structures can be constructed on a corbelled principle, such as stone chimney stacks, dovecotes or kilns.

**Corinthian** · See **Classical orders**. Distinguished by its capitals, which mimic acanthus leaves, and seen on both the north and south fronts at Kedleston, Mount Stewart's Temple of the Winds and Robert Adam's sumptuous Velvet Drawing Room at Saltram.

**Cornice** · Projecting uppermost band of a Classical entablature or, more generally, a projecting horizontal moulding that 'crowns' a structure or marks a junction within it, for example of an internal wall and ceiling.

*Right* · **Classical orders** illustrated in *A History of Architecture on the Comparative Method* (18th edition, 1975, page 1052) by Banister Fletcher.

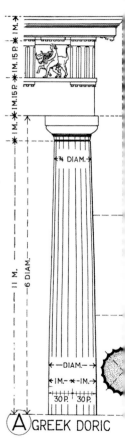

COMPARA

A GREEK DORIC

# VE PROPORTIONS of the ORDERS after SIR W. CHAMBERS

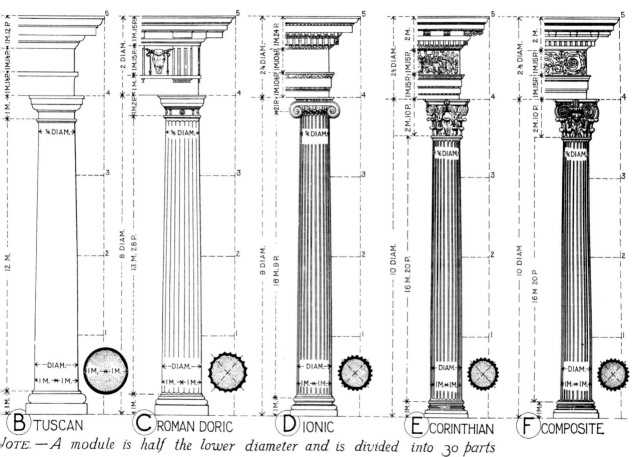

B TUSCAN    C ROMAN DORIC    D IONIC    E CORINTHIAN    F COMPOSITE

*NOTE.— A module is half the lower diameter and is divided into 30 parts*

**Cottage orné** · Designed rustic cottage, often within a picturesque landscape, such as Blaise Hamlet in Blaise Castle Park, a partnership between John Nash and Humphry Repton. Thatch, verandas, small ornamental openings and other 'cottagey' features are used to embellish the effect, as at Derrymore.

**Cross wing** · Addition to a structure at right angles to the original structure, often a medieval

*Above* · The stable block on the Wimpole Estate in Cambridgeshire, with its impressive **cupola**.

or Tudor hall, as at Lower Brockhampton. The cross wing typically housed private chambers or service rooms. At Alfriston Clergy House, a Wealden house, the cross wings are hidden beneath the main roof.

**Crow-stepped** · Stair-stepped decorative line along a gabled end, as in Castle Ward's Boathouse and Willington Dovecote, or to a parapet wall, as seen at Oxburgh.

**Cupola** · Dome or small turret placed on top of a structure for architectural effect, often supported on columns or posts and sometimes in combination with a bell, clock or viewing tower room. The original building at Quarry Bank has a cupola with a bell, and Wimpole's stables are adorned with a spectacularly tall example.

**Curtain wall** · Wall around a castle, connecting the towers or turrets and the gatehouse. Buildings and structures are often built against its inner, protected face, as at Bodiam. The term can also refer to the outer, non-load-bearing wall of a Modernist, framed building, such as The Homewood.

**Cusping** · Scalloped, curved cut-out edge to stone or timber, producing decorative lobes or a series of points. This is often seen alongside other decorative details, as at Little Moreton Hall, where the chevron, quatrefoil and cusped lozenge infill on the panelling is striking. Cusped window openings can be seen at Tyntesfield, Nymans and many other National Trust properties.

**Dais** · Low platform for a lectern or throne. Typically, medieval great halls such as Horton Court had a dais where the owner of the house would sit to hold court, take meals, or enjoy entertainment. Sometimes a canopy would be built above. The Great Hall dais platform survives at Chastleton.

**Decorated** · Style of Gothic architecture through the 13th and 14th centuries characterised by circular and curvilinear decorative forms in the bar tracery of windows, which became increasingly elaborate. The style is seen as revived by G.F. Bodley at St Mary's Chapel, Clumber.

**Dendrochronology** · Tree-ring dating to determine the age of construction timber. The analysis of patterns of growth rings, in comparison with known dated timbers, can be used to determine specific dates of felling, and therefore construction, due to the use of green (unseasoned) oak. Many National Trust places have been dated through dendrochronology, including Lower Brockhampton, Alfriston Clergy House, Aberconwy House and Springhill.

**Dentil** · One of a series of decorative rectangular blocks, tightly spaced to resemble a row of teeth.

**Doric** · *See* **Classical orders**

**Dutch gable** · High gable incorporating distinctive S-shaped (ogee) curves to the sides.

**Entablature** · Moulded section (including architrave, frieze and cornice) that runs horizontally across the tops of capitals in Classical architecture, often forming the base of a pediment, as at Nostell, Kedleston, Attingham and Castle Coole.

**Etruscan** · Inspired by the art of the Etruscan civilisation of central Italy, active between the

10th and 1st centuries BC. In the Theatre Royal at Bury St Edmunds, the figurative and flowing painted decoration resembles that found on Etruscan ceramics.

**Façade** · One of a building's external faces, typically the one that features the main entrance.

**Finial** · Upward-pointing decorative element at the top or corner of a structure such as a parapet, gate pier or gable, as seen along the roofline of Seaton Delaval, and atop the ridge at Nymans.

**Fluted** · Decorated with concave grooves carved or cast into the length of a shaft, column, etc. Often seen in Classical columns, as in the porch columns of John Nash's Llanerchaeron, or the slender cast-iron columns to Quarry Bank House's porch.

**Foliated** · Decorated with or imitating leaf forms.

**Frieze** · Band of horizontal decoration around a room. An exceptional plaster example is seen around the High Great Chamber at Hardwick. In Classical architecture, the middle portion of the entablature set above (or sometimes between) the capitals, as on the Ickworth rotunda.

**Garderobe** · Medieval latrine, often taking the form of a timber structure projecting beyond a masonry wall or a small chamber within the thickness of the stone walls of a castle, and

*Left* · Detail of the half-timbered medieval exterior of Lavenham Guildhall, Suffolk – an example of **jettying**.

discharging into a cesspit, castle moat, etc. Also sometimes used to refer to a closet for garments.

**Gothic Revival** · Architectural movement inspired by medieval architecture that began in the mid-18th century with a romantic interpretation of the style, more often referred to as Gothick. The movement gained momentum and increasingly pointed detailing through the 19th century. Followers, including G.F. Bodley at Powis and Clumber, William Burges at Knightshayes, and the Pugins (A.C. and A.W.N.) at Chirk, took the elements of medieval architecture and amplified or reinterpreted them. In Tyntesfield's Chapel, architect Arthur Blomfield took French Gothic as his inspiration.

**Gothick** · Largely interchangeable with Gothic Revival. Originating in England, it was a blend of Gothic design styles with a branch of Rococo and elements of Chinoiserie. It can be seen in Georgian architecture at Lacock Abbey and Plas Newydd.

**Grisaille** · Monochrome painting to imitate shallow relief sculpture, as seen in the Marble Hall at Kedleston and Attingham's Entrance Hall.

**Ionic** · *See* **Classical orders**

**Jettying** · Medieval and Tudor construction technique in which the upper storeys of a timber-framed building project beyond those below. This creates overhanging upper storeys and a protected walkway below, so that from a small footprint at ground-floor level a considerably larger house can be achieved above. Jettying can be seen at Lavenham Guildhall, Aberconwy House and Ightham Mote.

**Lime** · Mineral limestone is put through different processes (heating, hydrating) to change its chemical makeup in order to use it for various building purposes, such as in mortars, renders and paints. Lime-based materials are generally breathable, helping old buildings to dry out naturally without trapping moisture, and preventing mould growth internally. Until the 19th century, all buildings were constructed using lime mortars, renders and paints. The Romans even made a form of early concrete using lime and volcanic ash.

**Linenfold** · Tudor style of low-relief carving applied to timber panelling to imitate folded fabric, also found in 19th-century Gothic Revival buildings such as St Mary's Chapel, Clumber.

**Loggia** · Gallery for walking or sitting located behind an open colonnade or arcade, either as part of a building or as a separate structure, for example the Palladian bridge at Prior Park. At Seaton Delaval and Castle Coole, loggias flank the entrance front as linking passageways.

**Lozenge** · Diamond-shaped opening or space within timber-framing, as seen at Little Moreton Hall with cusping.

**Mullion and transom** · Substantial window frame bars running, respectively, vertically and horizontally between glazing. They are

*Above* · Decorated in an **Arts and Crafts** style, the **bull's eye** window at Red House, Bexleyheath, London, features William Morris's motto 'Si Je Puis' (If I Can).

principally medieval, Tudor and Jacobean in style, but were revived by the Arts and Crafts movement and so are commonly found in many suburban Victorian houses today. The building that pushed the boundaries, enabling extravagant amounts of glass to be used, is Hardwick Hall. Goddards in York is a 1920s Arts and Crafts revival example.

**Neo-classical** · Architectural style employing stylistic elements from Classical Greek and Roman architecture, such as a portico supported on columns, with decoration including swags, urns and sculpture. The Neo-classical style marked a reawakening of interest in all antique forms. Examples include Attingham Park, Hadrian's Arch at Shugborough and Stowe's Triumphal Arch.

*Below* · The carved **overmantel** in the Great Parlour at Speke Hall, Liverpool.

**Oeuil-de-boeuf or 'Bull's eye'** · Small round window often found in Classical architecture. A series appears in the stables at Tredegar as well as the Art and Crafts movement Red House, Bexleyheath.

**Ogee roof** · In section, a roof that culminates in a pointed apex with an S-shaped profile, as seen in the Montacute pavilions. Ogee curves occur widely in Renaissance architecture and are a feature of the Dutch-style gables that became fashionable in the 17th century, as seen at Blickling, and well into the 18th century with the Gothick trend, exemplified in Castle Ward's Gothick front.

**Overmantel** · Ornamental frame or decorative panel above the chimneypiece, forming the surround to the fireplace opening and often intended as a major architectural statement. The 16th century and 17th century saw some particularly beautiful and elaborate examples in polychromatic stone and plaster, such as those adorning Hardwick's fine rooms, Gawthorpe's Long Gallery, the King's Room at Godolphin and Dyffryn's Blue Drawing Room (where it was brought in from another location); and in carved wood, as in the Great Parlour at Speke Hall.

**Palladian** · Palladianism is a distinct sub-group of the Neo-classical, following the designs and style of Italian architect Andrea Palladio (1508–80), as captured in his *Quatro Libri dell' Archittetura* (Four Books of Architecture), published in 1570. Features include symmetry, seen in the grand façade at Nostell, and the rotunda, as at Wentworth Castle Gardens and Croome Court, as well as named imitations, such as Lyme's Palladian Courtyard and Prior Park Palladian Bridge.

**Parapet ·** Section of wall forming a low upstand that runs along the edge of a roof or the sides of a bridge. Often pierced and decorative like a balustrade, as at Lanhydrock, Montacute, Hardwick and Lodge Park.

**Pediment ·** In Classical architecture, a triangular or semi-circular gable, often forming the uppermost element of a portico or other opening.

**Perpendicular ·** Style of Gothic architecture that followed chronologically after Decorated, from the mid-14th through to the mid-15th century. Its name derives from the characteristic flatter arches and vertical lines on which the tracery, vaulting and window decoration are based, rather than the more flowing patterns previously seen. Lacock's cloister has some of England's finest Perpendicular tracery.

**Piano nobile ·** Italian Renaissance term for a building's principal storey containing its most important rooms, usually elevated over a lower floor to indicate its status. Typically accessed by a grand flight of steps, the *piano nobile* was often of greater height than the other storeys, giving higher ceilings to its reception rooms and further emphasising its significance externally.

**Pilaster ·** Narrow, projecting section of wall designed to give the architectural impression of a column set flush against a flat wall, or around a rotunda. The Mussenden Temple is wrapped in a cage of Ionic pilasters.

**Piloti ·** Modernist architectural detail in which slender columns are laid out in a grid pattern and support an upper storey. The term was coined by French Modernist architect Le Corbusier, whose Villa Savoie inspired Patrick Gwynne's The Homewood.

**Pinnacle ·** Sharply pointed stone or timber decorative finial. Associated with later medieval Gothic architecture, pinnacles are often seen on churches, such as St Mary's, Canons Ashby. Waddesdon's silhouette is highly decorated with pinnacles, as are Montacute's pavilions.

**Portico ·** Essentially an open porch, usually supported by a series of columns, stylistically borrowed from Classical temples such as the Parthenon, and a defining feature of the Neo-classical house as popularised during the 18th century. At Seaton Delaval, the portico is almost outsized, standing over two storeys high and providing a space from which to view the landscape. The earliest example in Britain is that added to The Vyne, *c.*1654.

*Right* · The earliest example of a Neo-classical **portico** (a porch supported by columns) in Britain is that added to The Vyne, Hampshire, *c.*1654.

**Proscenium** · Colonnade in front of a scene of buildings in Greek theatres, which became the model for modern theatre stages, as at the Theatre Royal in Bury St Edmunds, but also found as an architectural feature in houses, for example the Dining Room at Erddig, reworked by Thomas Hopper in 1826-7.

**Putlog** · Horizontal element of a historic timber scaffold. Putlog holes are recesses in the lower courses of masonry that supported the scaffolding timbers during construction. Commonly found in medieval buildings, they provide evidence of how the buildings were constructed. The great barn of Great Coxwell still displays putlog holes, as does Old Soar Manor.

**Quatrefoil** · Four-lobed feature defined by the cusping of stone tracery or timber framing in medieval and Gothic Revival architecture. It is generally used as an ornamental detail, as in the rich timber-framing of Little Moreton Hall and Rufford Old Hall, or as a window opening – as at Buckland Abbey.

**Quoin** · Dressed stone at the corners of a wall or building, often alternating between long and short, principally to create a strong corner and protect an otherwise potentially weak joint. Where a contrasting material is used or the quoins project from the wall surface, this becomes a decorative detail as well, as at Blickling, Uppark and Kingston Lacy.

*Above* · The exterior walls of Saltram House in Devon are covered in a thick layer of lime **render** known as **stucco**, the Italian word for 'plaster'.

**Ragstone** · Kentish Rag is a hard grey limestone, quarried in the Maidstone area and used for the construction of Knole. Elsewhere, 'rag' refers to stones quarried in thin pieces, typically used as flagstones.

**Renaissance** · Period in European history during which there was a cultural rebirth of Classical antiquity, principally from the ancient Greek and Roman civilisations, manifesting in great palaces such as those of the Medici. In England, the architectural and artistic expressions of this revival are visible from *c.*1550 in architectural masterpieces such as Knole, Montacute, Lyveden and Hardwick.

**Render** · A protective skin, often lime-based, applied to the exterior face of a wall. It can be relatively thin, such as coats of limewash to give breathable weather-proofing (as used since the Middle Ages on both timber-framed and masonry buildings). Natural pigments such as earth or animal blood were sometimes added, as at Treleddyd Fawr, or the mix left a natural white, as at Lower Brockhampton and Townend bank barn. More substantial renders, such as stucco, involve a thicker, smooth layer of lime render, fashionable in the 18th century and used at Ickworth, Saltram and Springhill. A roughcast includes aggregate to give a bumpy finish.

**Rosettes** · Decorative stone feature used throughout medieval architecture. The rosette is, as the name implies, a decorative ornament in the form of a rose, as seen around the 16th-century doorway at Horton Court, or in Claydon's staircase plasterwork.

**Rotunda** · Building that is circular in plan form, which if impractical to furnish is aesthetically and acoustically pleasing. A feature of Palladian-influenced architecture, rotundas can be found at Wentworth Castle Gardens, Ickworth, Mussenden Temple, Croome and Rievaulx Terrace.

**Roundel** · Small circular window or niche for sculpture, inscribed tablet, etc.

**Rustication** · Often used in Classical architecture, rusticated stonework is carved and patterned to appear more rugged and strong. An early English exponent was Inigo Jones at the Banqueting House in 1619, while John Vanbrugh used it to great effect a century later at Seaton Delaval. It was used for utilitarian structures and is commonly seen as a feature at basement storey, to give the illusion of a building emerging from bedrock. The rusticated gateway at Nunnington plays with an extreme form of rustication in combination with Neo-classical detailing.

**Sacristy** · The room in a church where sacred objects and vestments are kept. A large monastic sacristy survives at Lacock, a more modest Gothic Revival example can be seen at St Mary's Chapel, Clumber, and a tiny hidden sacristy survives at Baddesley Clinton.

**Scalloped** · Having an edge defined by semi-circular lines, giving a decorative profile or three-dimensional form, as in the 12th-century capitals flanking the south doorway to Horton Court. Large-scale scallop pattern is seen in the entablature of the Temple of Apollo at Stourhead, looping from one column to the next.

**Smoke-blackening** · In medieval halls, the fire would originally have been on a central, open hearth-stone rather than in a fireplace with a chimney. This meant that smoke had to escape through a purpose-built hole or louvre in the roof, as at Egryn, or simply to filter through gaps in the construction in simpler dwellings. This led to soot-staining of the roof timbers, which often survives in medieval hall houses even after they have been modernised and chimneys built, providing evidence of their ancient origins.

**Strapwork** · Decorative feature of Renaissance architecture also found in art and furniture and echoed in garden design. Decorative strapwork in stone can be seen in abundance at Hardwick and in the splendid stone screen in Montacute's Great Hall. Fine examples in plasterwork can be seen in the Long Gallery at Blickling, the work of Master Plasterer Edward Stanyon.

**Stucco** · Fine-quality render, often used over brickwork for a uniform finish or where the quality or availability of stone was insufficient. Stucco detailing is found in Osterley's portico and as the finish for the whole building at Saltram and Polesden Lacey.

**Swag** · Decorative device imitating cloth draped between two points (in contrast to the similar festoon, which represents garlands of flowers). A common feature in shallow relief Neo-classical plasterwork, restrained swags abound at Croome in the Adam Long Gallery and the

*Right* · **Tracery** in a window at Tyntesfield House, the **Gothic Revival** masterpiece near Bristol.

interior of the Rotunda. Swags range in execution from the daintily elegant Robert Adam ceilings at Saltram to the more robust stone in Blickling's entrance porch. An ebullient Rococo example can be seen in Sudbury's staircase plasterwork.

**Tambour doors** · Doors that are made from narrow slats, usually timber, as at The Homewood, or steel, and slide horizontally or vertically in grooves.

**Tithe barn** · Large medieval barn used to store the tithes (literally, one tenth of a farmer's crop) taken by the church or government as a tax. Tithe barns can be seen at Knole and Middle Littleton, Lacock and Great Coxwell.

**Tracery** · Intersecting decorative stone ribwork in vaulting or windows, creating geometric and flowing patterns, for example in the cloister at Lacock. A further example is hidden away in Lindisfarne Castle's undercroft, suggesting the space may formerly have been the chapel. It features widely in Gothic Revival buildings such as Knightshayes and Tyntesfield.

**Transept** · Projecting arms of a church building, adjoining the nave, as at Fountains Abbey.

**Tudor-Gothic** · Transitional phase between later medieval and Tudor architectural styles. More prevalent as the inspiration for revival domestic architecture, picking features from both medieval Gothic and Tudor periods, for example Cragside, and Crom boathouse.

**Tufa** · Rough, very lightweight building stone, commonly volcanic. In Classical design, tufa is often used to create architectural rustication in garden water features or grottoes. Found in the grottoes at Stowe and Croome.

**Tuscan** · *See* **Classical orders**. Roman order, from the Doric. Characterised by a simple entablature, column and rounded capital. Seen in the Nostell Obelisk Lodge and also at Erddig stables, dividing the stalls, and in the romantic ruins of the Orangery at Gibside.

**Tympanum** · The semi-circular or triangular face of a pediment, often decorated with sculpture. Also, an area above an opening that is contained by an arch.

**Undercroft** · Wholly or partially underground space such as a crypt beneath a church.

**Wattle and daub** · Type of wall infill made from strips of timber, known as withies, interwoven with staves and set within a structural frame. Daub, earth and lime-based renders are then applied to the timber structure, with the addition of animal hair, straw and other fibrous materials to reinforce the mix. Frequently found in timber-framed medieval houses such as Aberconwy, Lower Brockhampton and Little Moreton Hall.

*Compiled by Dr Elizabeth Green,*
*Simon Robertshaw and David Boulting*

# Index

# Acknowledgements

The author is immensely grateful to George Clarke for his enthusiastic introduction and to those colleagues who contributed entries to this book: Frances Bailey (Senior National Curator), Rupert Goulding (Acting Head Curator), James Grasby (Building & Landscape Design Adviser), Sally-Anne Huxtable (former Head Curator), Mark Newman (Archaeologist), Stephen Ponder (Cultural Heritage Curator), Lucy Porten (Senior National Curator), George Roberts (Cultural Heritage Curator), Simon Robertshaw (Building & Landscape Design Adviser) and Emma Slocombe (Senior National Curator). Together, we owe a debt of gratitude to all those whose past research, recording and analysis have provided the foundation for this publication. National Trust Heritage Records, Conservation Management Plans, Historic Buildings Surveys and Vernacular Building Surveys have been heavily drawn upon, and represent decades of accrued knowledge about the historic buildings of the National Trust. The listed building databases of Cadw, Northern Ireland Historic Environment Division and Historic England have also provided invaluable information. The conservation skills and dedication of those who maintain and repair the buildings in the care of the Trust, preserving our heritage, are warmly recognised.

The author also gratefully acknowledges the many members of National Trust staff who have made this book possible, including the cultural heritage curators, property curators and collections and house managers who checked and corrected the entries. In particular, Simon Robertshaw must be thanked for his substantial contribution to the glossary.

*60 Remarkable Buildings* is the first book in this series to be translated into Welsh, with advice and support from Lhosa Daly (Regional Director, Wales), Haf Davies (Communications and Marketing Consultant) and Lottie Mazhindu (Consultancy Manager); and harnessing the creativity and linguistic brilliance of Steffan Rhys Williams, who translated the text into Welsh – *Diolch yn fawr*.

The process of writing this book has been made entirely pleasurable due to working with such patient and generous colleagues, in particular Christopher Tinker, the National Trust's Publisher for Curatorial Content, who commissioned this book and oversaw the editing, design and production; and David Boulting, Editor in the Cultural Heritage Publishing team, who was the project editor and contributed entries to the glossary.

We are grateful to Matthew Young for his wonderful cover design; Anjali Bulley and Beryl Griffiths for proofreading the book so meticulously; Dr J. Graham Jones and Christopher Phipps for their indexing; and Richard Deal at Dexter Premedia for the origination. We would also like to thank photographers Leah Band, David Cordner and John Miller for new photography of several of the featured buildings and sites, and the property teams for supporting the shoots.

The National Trust gratefully acknowledges a generous bequest from the late Mr and Mrs Kenneth Levy that has supported the cost of preparing this book through the Trust's Cultural Heritage Publishing programme.

## THE AUTHORS

**Dr Elizabeth Green** is the National Trust's Senior National Curator for Architectural History and for Wales and has been a curator within the National Trust, in Wales and Northern Ireland, since 2002. Previously, she spent eight years in private practice specialising in historic building analysis and adaptive reuse. Her principal interests lie in medieval, vernacular and Welsh architecture, on which subjects she has written widely.

**George Clarke** is an architect, television presenter, campaigner and educator. In 2020, despite the challenges presented by the first Covid-19 lockdown, he recorded the Channel 4 television series *George Clarke's National Trust Unlocked*, screened later that year. His other popular television series include *Restoration Man*, *George Clarke's Amazing Spaces* and *Old House, New Home*.

# Picture credits

Pages 2, 4–5, 9, 14, 28, 64–5, 81, 96–7, 120, 168–9 © National Trust Images/Andrew Butler • 6 © Amazing Productions • 8, 18, 70–1, 102–3, 108–9, 121, 150–1, 161, 166, 192–3, 206–7 © National Trust Images/John Millar • 10 © National Trust Images/Tom Carr • 12, 30, 125, 144–5, 152–3, 153, 178–9, 186 © National Trust Images/John Miller • 15, 78–9, 186 © National Trust Images/Mark Bolton • 16–17, 22–3, 24, 36–7, 56, 69, 110, 134, 154–5, 157, 170 © National Trust Images/Chris Lacey • 20, 188–9, 190–1 © National Trust Images/Stuart Cox • 25 © National Trust Images/Alison Marsh • 26–7 © National Trust Images/Oliver Benn • 29 © National Trust Images/Sylvaine Poitau • 31, 42–3, 44–5, 54–5, 106–7, 129, 130, 131 © National Trust Images/Robert Morris • 32–3 © National Trust Images/Sam Milling • 34–5, 58, 67, 72–3, 80, 84–5, 88–9, 117, 171, 174–5, 176, 177 © National Trust Images/James Dobson • 38–9, 136, 138, 160 © National Trust Images/Matthew Antrobus • 40, 41, 52, 126, 127 © National Trust Images/Mike Selby • 46, 76–7, 104, 112, 147, 156, 201, 209 © National Trust Images/Andreas von Einsiedel • 47 © National Trust Images/Mike Calnan/Chris Lacey • 49 © National Trust Images/Phil Neagle • 50–1 © National Trust Images/Derek Croucher • 53 © National Trust Images/Richard Scott • 57 (left), 148 © National Trust Images • 57 (right), 139, 140, 141, 142 © National Trust Images/John Hammond • 59 © National Trust Images/Derrick E. Witty • 60–1 © National Trust Images/Paul Mogford • 62, 146 © National Trust Images/Paul Harris • 63 © National Trust Images/Paul Wakefield • 66, 101, 208 © National Trust Images/Nadia Mackenzie • 68 © Historic Images/Alamy Stock Photo • 74–5 Crown copyright/Permission of RCAHMW under delegated authority from The Keeper of Public Records • 82–3 © National Trust/Mike Henton • 86–7 © Andrew Lloyd/Alamy Stock Photo • 87 © National Trust • 90 © National Trust Images/Colin Davison • 91, 115 © National Portrait Gallery, London • 92, 94–5, 172–3 © National Trust/Christopher Tinker • 93 © National Trust Images/David Noton • 98–9, 132–3, 137, 149, 182, 210–11 © National Trust Images/Arnhel de Serra • 100, 204, 212 © National Trust Images/Rupert Truman • 105 © Angela Serena Gilmour/Alamy Stock Photo • 111 © National Trust Images/David Watson • 113, 114, 180–1 © National Trust Images/David Cordner • 116 © National Trust Images/David Levenson • 118–19 © National Trust Images/Rob Skinner • 122 © Artokoloro/Alamy Stock Photo • 123 © Bildarchiv Monheim GmbH/Alamy Stock Photo • 124, 184, 185 © National Trust Images/Dennis Gilbert • 128 Ordnance Survey, 1888 • 135 © National Trust Images/Ian Shaw • 143 © National Trust Images/Will Webster • 158–9 © National Trust Images/Roger Coulam • 162–3 © Waddesdon Image Library/Stuart Bebb • 164 © National Trust Images/Hugh Mothersole • 165 © Waddesdon Image Library/John Bigelow Taylor • 167 © National Trust Images/Leah Band • 183 © Mike Cadwallader • 187 National Trust/Kirk & Sons • 194, 195 © National Trust/Jemma Finch • 196–7 © Heneghan Peng Architects/Marie-Louise Halpenny • 198–9 © Heneghan Peng Architects/Hufton + Crow • 202–3 © RIBA Collections • 214 © National Trust Images/Stephen Robson

*Front cover, clockwise from top left:* Willington Dovecote © National Trust Images/Mike Selby • Mussenden Temple © National Trust Images/Bernie Brown • Horsey Windpump © National Trust Images/Justin Minns • Penrhyn Castle © National Trust Images/Annapurna Mellor • Obelisk Lodge, Nostell © National Trust Images/Chris Lacey • Little Moreton Hall © National Trust Images/Paul Harris • *Back cover, clockwise from top left:* Souter Lighthouse © National Trust Images/Annapurna Mellor • Bodiam Castle © National Trust Images/Matthew Antrobus • Blickling Hall © National Trust Images/Andrew Butler • Lyveden New Bield © National Trust Images/Paul Wakefield • Oast Houses, Sissinghurst © National Trust/Christopher Tinker • Great Coxwell © National Trust Images/Robert Morris

Published in Great Britain by the National Trust, Heelis,
Kemble Drive, Swindon, Wiltshire SN2 2NA

National Trust Cultural Heritage Publishing

ISBN 978-0-70-780465-1 (English edition)
ISBN 978-0-70-780466-8 (Welsh edition)

A CIP catalogue record for this book is available from the British Library.

10 9 8 7 6 5 4 3 2 1

Publisher: Christopher Tinker · Project editor: David Boulting ·
Translator: Steffan Rhys Williams (Welsh edition) · Proofreaders:
Anjali Bulley (English edition); Beryl Griffiths (Welsh edition)
Indexers: Christopher Phipps (English edition); Dr J. Graham Jones
(Welsh edition) · Cover designer: Matthew Young ·
Page design concept: Peter Dawson, www.gradedesign.com

Colour origination by Dexter Premedia Ltd, London
Printed in Wales by Gomer Press Ltd on FSC-certified paper

Measurements are given in metric form except where imperial units, such
as miles and acres, will be more familiar to UK readers (1 mile = 1.6 kilometres,
1 acre = 0.4 hectares)

Discover the wealth of our collections – great art and
treasures to see and enjoy throughout England, Wales
and Northern Ireland. Visit the National Trust website:
www.nationaltrust.org.uk/art-and-collections
and the National Trust Collections website:
www.nationaltrustcollections.org.uk

## ALSO AVAILABLE IN THIS SERIES

*125 Treasures from the Collections
of the National Trust*
ISBN 978-0-70-780453-8

*100 Paintings from the Collections
of the National Trust*
ISBN 978-0-70-780460-6

*50 Great Trees of the National Trust*
ISBN 978-0-70-780461-3

*100 Curiosities & Inventions from the
Collections of the National Trust*
ISBN 978-0-70-780462-0

*100 Books from the Libraries
of the National Trust*
ISBN 978-0-70-780464-4